# Maximize Life By Living For Peace, Harmony, And Joy

# Maximize Life By Living For Peace, Harmony, And Joy

Dr. Robert H. Schram

Copyright © 2006 by Dr. Robert H. Schram.

| | | |
|---|---|---|
| Library of Congress Number: | | 2005903262 |
| ISBN: | Hardcover | 1-4134-9312-2 |
| | Softcover | 1-4134-9311-4 |

All rights reserved. No part of this book may be reproduced, stored in a retrieval system, or transmitted by any means, electronic, mechanical, photocopying, recording, or otherwise, without written permission from the author.

This book was printed in the United States of America.

To order additional copies of this book, contact:
Xlibris Corporation
1-888-795-4274
www.Xlibris.com
Orders@Xlibris.com
28356

# Contents

ACKNOWLEDGMENTS ................................................ xiii
INTRODUCTION ........................................................ xv

A CAN-DO ATTITUDE ................................................... 1
A PERSON WILL ACHIEVE ............................................. 3
A THOUGHT IS ............................................................ 5
ACCENTUATE THE POSITIVE .......................................... 7
ACQUISITION ............................................................. 9
ACTING ON THINGS ................................................... 11
ALL MOMENTS ARE SPECIAL ........................................ 13
ALL WHO LIVE ARE RICH ............................................ 15
ALLOW THE INTENSITY OF EXPERIENCE ........................ 17
ALLOW TIME TO BE YOUR BEST FRIEND ....................... 19
ALWAYS TAKE THE TIME TO DEAL ................................ 21
ARE YOU CURSED BY CHANGE? ................................... 23
AT THE END OF THE DAY ............................................ 25
AVOIDANCE .............................................................. 27
BE HELPFUL .............................................................. 29
BE SOMEONE ............................................................ 31
BE SPECIFIC ABOUT YOUR WANTS ............................... 33
BE TRUE TO SELF AND OTHERS ................................... 35
BE YOUR OWN PERSON .............................................. 37
BECOME JOYFUL ....................................................... 39
BEING KIND .............................................................. 41
BEING PRESENT ........................................................ 43
BEING UPSET ............................................................ 45
BLAMING OTHERS ..................................................... 47
BOUNCING BACK ...................................................... 49
BREATHE IN AND OUT ............................................... 51

| | |
|---|---|
| BRING ALL YOUR POTENTIAL TO LIFE | 53 |
| BRING OUT THE BEST IN OTHERS | 55 |
| CHALLENGES | 57 |
| CHOOSE TO CHANGE | 59 |
| COMMITMENT | 61 |
| COMPREHENSION | 63 |
| CONFLICT | 65 |
| CONTINUAL MOVEMENT | 67 |
| CRITICISM | 69 |
| CURIOSITY AND EXPLORATION | 71 |
| DESIRES | 73 |
| DISSATISFACTION | 75 |
| DO NOT ALLOW DOUBT | 77 |
| DO THE THINGS THAT GIVE JOY | 79 |
| DON'T SWEAT THE SMALL STUFF | 81 |
| EACH MOMENT IS AN OPPORTUNITY | 83 |
| EACH MOMENT... NOT TO BE SQUANDERED | 85 |
| EFFORT PAYS | 87 |
| EVERY MOMENT IS GOOD | 89 |
| EVERYTHING YOU DO MATTERS | 91 |
| EVERYTHING YOU NEED YOU HAVE | 93 |
| EXERCISE CONTROL OVER ACTIONS | 95 |
| FACING YOUR FEARS | 97 |
| FAILURE IS HELPFUL | 99 |
| FEEL GOOD AND MAKE GOOD | 101 |
| FEELING IS NOT WHO YOU ARE | 103 |
| FOCUS ON SELF | 105 |
| FOCUSING ON THE POSITIVE | 107 |
| FOLLOW THROUGH | 109 |
| FOLLOW YOUR DREAMS | 111 |
| FOR EVERY ACT OF VIOLENCE | 113 |
| GENUINE HAPPINESS | 115 |
| GIVING THE EXTRA EFFORT | 117 |
| GOING WITH WHAT WORKS | 119 |
| GOOD LISTENING | 121 |
| GRATITUDE | 123 |

| | |
|---|---|
| HABITS | 125 |
| HAPPINESS IS ALREADY YOURS | 127 |
| HOW YOU USE YOUR TIME | 129 |
| IMAGINATION | 131 |
| IMPROVING | 133 |
| IT IS A WIN-WIN SITUATION | 135 |
| IT IS ALL ABOUT THE PROCESS | 137 |
| KNOW YOURSELF | 139 |
| KEEP AN OPEN MIND | 141 |
| LEARN FROM FAILURE | 143 |
| LET PERSISTENCE GUIDE YOU | 145 |
| LETTING GO OF EGO | 147 |
| LIFE IS A SERIES | 149 |
| LIFE REQUIRES ADAPTATION | 151 |
| LIVE A WORRY FREE LIFE | 153 |
| LIVE BEFORE YOU DIE | 155 |
| LIVE LIFE SINCERELY | 157 |
| LIVING LIFE IS UP TO YOU | 159 |
| LIVING A POSITIVE LIFE | 161 |
| LOVE LASTS | 163 |
| MAKE A PRESCRIPTION | 165 |
| MAKING ERRORS | 167 |
| MAKING THE BEST FROM THE WORST | 169 |
| MASTERPIECE | 171 |
| MOMENTS OFFER IT ALL | 173 |
| MUSCLES | 175 |
| NEED | 177 |
| NEGATIVE HABITS | 179 |
| NO DAY IS A BAD DAY | 181 |
| YOU—NOW IS THE KEY | 183 |
| OPPORTUNITY | 185 |
| OPPORTUNITY THAT CHALLENGES | 187 |
| OTHER PEOPLE MIRROR YOU | 189 |
| OUR ABILITIES | 191 |
| PASSION | 193 |
| PATIENCE | 195 |

PEOPLE COME AND GO ............................................................ 197
PEOPLE WHO HELP YOU ...................................................... 199
PERFECTIONISM ....................................................................... 201
PERSEVERE .................................................................................. 203
PLANNING IS IMPORTANT BUT ........................................ 205
POSITIVE PEOPLE ..................................................................... 207
REALITY IS WHAT IS ............................................................... 209
REGARDLESS HOW HIGH THE GOAL ........................... 211
REPEATING GOOD .................................................................. 213
RESPONSIBILITY ....................................................................... 215
SUCCESS IS NOT MONEY, FAME, AND POWER ........ 217
SUCCESS NEEDS FAILURE .................................................... 219
TAKE A HIGHER PERSPECTIVE .......................................... 221
TAKE DOWN YOUR PSYCHIC WALL ............................. 223
TAKE LIFE IN THE PRESENT ................................................ 225
TAKING CARE OF YOURSELF ............................................. 227
TASK COMPLETION ............................................................... 229
THE BEST TIME TO BE POSITIVE ...................................... 231
THE BIG PICTURE .................................................................... 233
THERE'S A REASON ................................................................ 235
THE WORLD DOES NOT OWE YOU .............................. 237
THE WORLD IS FULL .............................................................. 239
THERE IS ALWAYS HOPE ..................................................... 241
THINKING AND ACTING ..................................................... 243
THIS IS YOUR BIG MOMENT .............................................. 245
THIS MOMENT YOU CAN DECIDE .................................. 247
THOUGHTS ARE POWERFUL .............................................. 249
TRANQUILITY ........................................................................... 251
TURN IT AROUND .................................................................. 253
USE TIME TO ACCOMPLISH ............................................... 255
WE ALL CAN GET IN THE GAME ..................................... 257
WE ALL HAVE GIFTS .............................................................. 259
WE LIVE WITH CHANGE ...................................................... 261
WE TAKE OTHERS BY LISTENING AND FEELING .. 263
WHAT YOU GIVE IS WHAT YOU GET ........................... 265
WHEN YOU ARE STUCK ....................................................... 267

| | |
|---|---|
| WHAT'S HOLDING YOU BACK? | 269 |
| WHENEVER YOU FALL | 271 |
| WHEREVER YOU GO BE KIND | 273 |
| WHETHER YOUR GOALS ARE BIG OR SMALL | 275 |
| WORDS ARE IMPORTANT | 277 |
| WORKING IS IMPORTANT | 279 |
| YOU ARE ALIVE | 281 |
| YOU DESERVE THE BEST | 283 |
| YOU HAVE THE POWER | 285 |
| YOUR CAPABILITIES | 287 |
| YOUR DREAMS | 289 |
| YOUR EXPECTATIONS | 291 |
| YOUR EYES | 293 |
| YOUR INFLUENCE | 295 |
| YOUR LIFE'S DIRECTION | 297 |
| YOUR POTENTIAL | 299 |
| YOUR VIEW | 301 |
| ZOOMING TO DESTINY | 303 |
| MAY PEACE AND JOY BE WITH YOU | 305 |

## DEDICATION

This book is dedicated to my loving soul mate, wise
partner, and a truly beautiful woman,
Jean Lou Kyerubach;

to my sons,
Aaron and Justin,
Who continue to inspire me to live every moment fully;

in loving memory of my wife,
Shirley Meyers Schram, who worked tirelessly on behalf
of others;

and in loving memory of my parents,
William Saul Schram and Fay Tabolsky-Schram,
for a lifetime of love and encouragement.

# ACKNOWLEDGMENTS

I thank and acknowledge my partner and *"bashert"* Jean Lou Ryersbach, who has played a major role in my evolution as a human being through her kind, supportive, and insightful presence.

I thank my sons Aaron and Justin for all the years of pure pleasure they gave me, being with them, and seeing them mature into sensitive adult human beings.

I thank my wife, Shirley Schram, may she rest in peace, for her years of love and dedication to my sons and me.

I thank my sister, Lynne McCabe, and her husband Ralph, for being available during my darkest periods of depression.

I thank Ralph S. Marston, Jr. for his book "The Daily Motivator To Go" (Image Express Inc. Austin, TX 1997) for providing many insights on positive living.

I thank Marta Kaufmann for her friendship and insight regarding a book title.

I thank my editor Roberta Israeloff for her dedication of time and energy.

# INTRODUCTION

My journey began in Newark, NJ in 1946, as the first-born son of a psychiatrist father and poetic mother. When my sister Lynne was two, we moved first to Bloomfield, and then to Westfield, NJ. Our parents had a laissez-faire attitude toward us. They didn't express love and affection easily or openly—only sporadic pride in my accomplishments on the soccer or baseball field. There were few discussions and little interaction in our family. I spent many hours alone in my room, ruminating and entertaining myself, disconnected from my feelings.

As the class clown through high school and college, I treasured the joy of laughter, a gift I inherited from my mother. Though I started college as an engineering major, I dropped out after my first semester to become a liberal arts major, graduating with a BA in Political Science and a MA in Personnel and Counseling. I was career counseled into human services and, after failing my Army physical, I took a number of jobs in New York and New Jersey. In 1971, when I was twenty-five, I married one of my college classmates, Shirley Meyers, and we soon had two beautiful sons . . . Aaron, who was born in 1975, and Justin, born two years later.

As Shirley and I focused our energy on raising our sons and developing our careers, my feelings of disconnection persisted. The years leading up to my sons' Bar Mitzvahs, however, opened me up to the universe of the spirit, albeit the intellectual side of that universe. In my forties, after my son Aaron was seriously injured while riding his bicycle, I filled myself with food, Jewish history, Talmud, and the pursuit of my doctorate in Public Administration, which I received from Nova University in 1995. Within months of Justin's birth, I was fortunate to be selected for my dream job... Executive Director of BARC in Bucks County, PA (1977-present), a nonprofit serving people with developmental disabilities.

Loving my job and keeping busy with family activities... little league, soccer league, swimming teams, marching band, karate, music lessons, Shirley's township events, and our struggling thirty family synagogue... kept me going, but did little to ameliorate the symptoms of clinical depression that grew over time. I was wallowing in a morass of symptoms accentuated by denial. Though I worked in the mental health field, I couldn't help myself. It was only when the symptoms became too much to bear, in my late forties, that I sought and received help. Aaron and Justin were both attending college at that time, leaving me to face the stark deficiencies of my marriage. Shirley and I didn't have any real connection to each other; our mutual respect had withered over the years, and we shared few mutual interests. As I began my sixth decade, we separated. During the separation and divorce proceedings, I moved to Bucks County, PA.

One day, I asked Jean Ryersbach, to lunch. She was a twenty-year professional acquaintance I had met via Bucks County United Way meetings. As fate would have it, I ended up renting a room in her house. Within a month, I went from tenant to soul mate and partner.

It was only after another serious bout with depression that I found yoga and meditation, which has led me to teach and develop my own school of yoga and meditation, anchored by Judaic spiritual tradition and practice. I feel as if I've discovered many feelings that have been hidden from me until now, as well as a deep connection to G-d and to other people. In this, Jean has been my inspiration.

My journey through life inspired and moved me to write this book . . . to reveal and expose, freely and openly, who I am, and what I have experienced, in the hope that you will be similarly inspired and moved to document your journey on each page. I believe that understanding who we really are is at the core of living a more fulfilling and joyous life.

As you will see, each chapter is two pages in length. The first section explains why the concept is important to leading a more joyful life. The second section relates how the concept relates to my personal journey, and the third section is for you to write . . . to relate your personal experience.

Our life's journey begins at birth and ends with death; it is always evolving. When you write your personal experience, take time to consider your strengths and weaknesses in each particular concept area. Use your time not only to read, but also to grow and develop a more comprehensive understanding of who you are and areas that you may want to enhance and expand. As I wrote, I developed a clearer understanding of who I am and had insight into areas I would like to further explore.

You'll also discover your own pace for reading this book. You may choose to read and write about only one chapter a day, or you may read half the book in one sitting. Like living, the important thing is that you enjoy the journey!

Read, think, write, and enjoy!

# A CAN-DO ATTITUDE

A can-do attitude is how you get things done. If you believe that anything is possible, then the whole world of possibilities opens up to you. If, however, you believe something can never be achieved, then you insure that it never will.

Simply believing it can be done puts you well on the way to doing it. Many people, for example, thought it was impossible for man to fly but the Wright Brothers traveled to Kitty Hawk believing otherwise. Many people thought the Soviet Union would last forever; today, it no longer exists.

Doubt is easy; positive belief takes effort. Transform your doubt to a belief that you will achieve, and . . . voila! Your life will flow graciously and joyfully.

ME—When I was in my late forties and early fifties I had a deep sense of worthlessness, a feeling that I was incapable of doing anything. Through yoga, meditation, psychotherapy, and experimentation with several anti-depressants, all the symptoms of depression finally lifted but only after about five years. I realized how unrealistic my sense of hopelessness was, and I was able to revert back to the carefree "can-do" attitude of my youth when nothing seemed unrealistic or beyond my reach. Now, though older, more mature and less carefree, I nonetheless am able to realistically embrace "can-do" as a motto for doing the things that are important to me.

YOU—

# A PERSON WILL ACHIEVE

A person will achieve greatness if he or she is willing. A person will take an idea and make it happen. A person will develop his dreams. A person will reach for the heavens. A person will make life work every moment of every day. A person will enjoy herself every moment that she is alive. A person will do all the things that he ever wanted to do. A person will know that this moment is the first moment of the rest of her life and should not be wasted. A person will relish all that life has to offer. A person will know love and express it often. A person will know gratitude and be grateful. A person will shine throughout the universe.

This person could and should be you . . . it is simply and entirely up to you.

ME—As a first-born child, I was raised by parents who allowed me to pursue whatever I wanted with very limited guidance from them. Because I always felt I had my parents' support, I grew up to become a very—perhaps excessively—self-confident person. I never challenged my own greatness.

But becoming great, however one defines greatness, is a life-long journey. For me it has always involved much more than social, familial, and employment success. Fundamentally, it is about how much I love me and how I am able to affect, guide, and help others.

YOU—

# A THOUGHT IS

A thought is in your mind right now. Is it a good one? If not, make it one that will change the world and bring enlightenment and joy to you and all creatures.

Do you fret away your precious moments with errant, negative thoughts? Is your mind filled with self-defeating worry and concern? Come back to the positive. Give your mind a special treat by turning your concentration to all the gifts you have at this moment. Do it each and every moment of every day. Do it now . . . because this is the last opportunity you will have for this moment, right now.

ME—It took me fifty years to realize that "worry" was my best friend, and another five years to obtain a divorce from this friend. Only when I was finally free of worry was I able to start to love myself and became connected to everything around me, especially in nature. I still have some miles to travel on the road to deeper spiritual connection to other people. This involves letting go of all my protective barriers—ego-preservation, self-protection, passive aggressiveness, and intellectualism. My ego makes me selfish and judgmental of people, places and things; it works hard at protection and defensiveness. Growing up in a quiet household with scant expression of emotion, I never really connected to anger but rather learned to express it only by quietly agitating others.

YOU—

# ACCENTUATE THE POSITIVE

"Accentuate the positive," the old song tells us—and if you do, your life will become happier and the world a better place.

No matter how difficult a circumstance may be, it's finite; it has a beginning and an end. Your dreams, however, have no end. Your dreams are always higher and bigger than your present challenges. When you accentuate the positive, you turn the circumstantial negatives in your life into what they always have been—short-lived, circumstantial challenges.

Sometimes you'll discover your appreciation of positive connection with animals and plants before you can connect to people. That is fine. The quality of the connection is what counts.

ME—During some of the darkest periods of my life—when a truck hit my twelve-year-old son Aaron, when I was struggling through a difficult marriage—I found it very difficult to accentuate the positive. It was much easier for me to retreat into a cave and withdraw from the world. But the more I withdrew, the more I spiraled downward into depression. After many years, I was able to slowly come out of my cave. I first connected to animals, plants, and the beauty of nature. My ability to connect with other people took time. But as I evolved, I developed a more involved and meaningful social existence, one that wasn't only related to work. A few years later, I faced yet another challenge: as my two sons matured and became increasingly independent, I was no longer able to take refuge in living and doing just for them. I was forced to live and do for myself. Slowly, I rediscovered the ability to appreciate each moment and the miracle of life itself.

YOU—

# ACQUISITION

The acquisition of things does not make for happiness; it only results in our having more things. Many people convince themselves that they do not have enough. All they want is more, never taking the time to appreciate what they have.

Do not allow possessiveness and ownership to be your goal and end-all. We come into this world with nothing and leave it with nothing . . . so what is the great rush to possess? For what purpose? For what end? Whatever energy you put into acquisition takes away from the energy needed to be present, to be grateful for all that you naturally have, as a gift. Let go of your need to pursue acquiring things and come fully into the light of living.

Have you ever taken a moment to marvel at indoor plumbing? Hot water? Electricity? If not, why not? Are you too busy contemplating what you still need? Are you dreaming of having the newest product on the market?

When was the last time you appreciated the colors in the sky as the sun set? Or the sound of water rushing in a stream. Or the way a ripe tomato tastes in your mouth. Do you appreciate and take pleasure and joy in the miraculous gifts of our senses? We come into the world with nothing and that's how we leave. What is so critical about accumulating things we cannot take with us after we die, when we return to the earth?

ME—As the child of parents who lived through America's Great Depression, I was instilled with frugality and an appreciation for what we had: a nice home, plenty of food, good schools, two modest cars, air conditioning, heat, televisions, and stereos. Like my parents, I have never had the need to acquire more than I actually needed and knew the importance of education, a safe and secure dwelling, good food and transportation. I provided these things for my family but stayed clear of fashionable and upscale purchases. My ultimate liberation from possessions came after my divorce when I gave up my house, all furnishings, all electronics, and my car. I drive a company owned car, have clothing, and subsidize the support of Jean's home. I developed an even greater appreciation for many of the things I once took for granted . . . like heat in the winter and cold drinks in the summer . . . after visiting other countries. The joy I feel from sensing, living and giving to others is much more important to me than acquisitions. Each day I focus on my G-d given gifts rather than concerning myself with all the things I do not have. Tranquility and inner peace is much more important to me than driving a new car. I love the feel of a warm shower in the morning followed by a refreshing cold dousing. I love the smell and feel of the air as I leave the house, be it cold, warm, bright, wet, dry, damp, or gray. I love to watch and hear birds, and animals any time. I love the smell of freshly cut grass, the softness of a baby's face.

YOU—

# ACTING ON THINGS

Acting on things, rather than dwelling on them, is the key to feeling better. Most of the things we think about acting on are not so difficult or complex that we can't come up with a plan to accomplish them. And by not acting we insure that things will remain incomplete.

Anything you are worried about can be resolved by acting on it. Most assuredly, whatever you are worried about is more likely to become reality through inaction. If your path is impassable, find another path to travel. If your decision to act is painful, just imagine how much more pain you will engender through worry and passivity. The critical difference between wishing and doing always involves some sort of activity. By acting on something, you insure that it will be.

ME—As the first-born child, six years older than my sister, I was granted the freedom to explore and do things that I wanted to do, within reason. My freedom to explore, and learn for myself enhanced my self-confidence—and this remains true even though I have failed many more times than I have succeeded. My success has always come through action. For example, I was rejected from 95% of the jobs to which I applied. But I continued to work and apply for the job of my dreams, something that would challenge, intrigue, and hold my interest. Over the course of ten years and after at least five jobs, I was named Executive Director of BARC (a nonprofit organization providing supports for people with developmental disabilities), a job that perfectly matched my skills, experience, background, and upbringing. This position provided me with a career that will last until my retirement. And I achieved it not through passivity but by taking action.

YOU—

# ALL MOMENTS ARE SPECIAL

All moments are special because you only have one time to experience it. Because life is special and extraordinary, it follows that each moment of life is special and extraordinary. Each moment presents an abundance of good and wonderful richness. Open up your heart, look around you, feel the presence of the moment, flow with it, be with it, go with it as far as your imagination will take you. There is no limit to each moment's possibilities and they are here, right now, for you to enjoy.

If your moments have not been special, it is never too late to change your path. Break free from the emotional prison in which you're living. All it takes to enjoy yourself in gratitude and joy is the will to change your life from this day forward. You need not postpone this vision of life until "one day," or consider it a farfetched fantasy. Your life of joy is available to you right now! Just find a way to take the first step.

ME—During my adolescence and during my third decade, when I was in my twenties, despite having pimples and being obsessed with sex—I enjoyed most every moment without really understanding that my enjoyment was what life was all about. Now that I'm in my sixth decade, I really do understand that life is all about the simple daily moments. I try to be in the flow, and to rise to every moment with joy and gratitude. In the more challenging moments of meeting a deadline, or dealing with an injury or death, I do my best to concentrate on the flow of living, with all it's inevitable ups and downs. I use the calming mantra of knowing that, over longer period of time, things do work themselves out.

YOU—

# ALL WHO LIVE ARE RICH

All who live are rich. Wealth is not about having assets or money; richness is not about accumulating wealth. It is about being in touch with who you are and your appreciation for all you have: your senses, your experiences, your knowledge, your caring and loving feelings, and your understanding.

Those who are most wealthy are those who appreciate what they have, and are eager to share it. They know they are alive. The source of their wealth isn't material; rather, it derives from their grateful spirits.

ME—Though I have never coveted possessions, I nonetheless have spent most of my adult life earning and saving money so I could live comfortably in retirement and old age. In my early fifties after my sons' graduations from college, I realized that the need to keep saving was no longer necessary—I had enough accumulated in my pension account and my personal saving to live reasonably, especially with social security retirement income. Today, I am simply appreciative for all that I have. Instead of worrying about material savings, I appreciate my senses, my sentience, my abilities, and just being alive.

YOU—

# ALLOW THE INTENSITY OF EXPERIENCE

Allow the intensity of your experience be part of who you are. Each moment of each day, you experience life: some good, some bad, and some in-between. Cherish all of these moments by allowing them to fill you up with the satisfaction that each moment is a precious gift. The good moments should be embraced each glorious second while the bad and in-between should be fully experienced so as to learn and grow. Everything you experience becomes part of who you are.

At the same time, know when to decrease the intensity or to let it go completely. While it's critically important to move forward in your life and achieve all you want, life is ultimately about sharing with others. That which you can obtain only by hurting others is not worth the pain.

Allowing and welcoming intensity doesn't mean becoming aggressive. And being intense does not mean holding on to things so tenaciously that no one is able to share in the joy. Know how to relate to all that life has to offer. Let all your treasured experiences become heart-felt and alive so you can move into an even more exciting and a more treasured future.

ME—All the experiences of my life, both my achievements and my suffering, are part of who I am. I am very proud that in all my experiences I have never deliberately hurt others or deliberately used others for my own self-aggrandizement. I still have a lot to learn about releasing my protective barriers of ego preservation, self-protection, passive aggressiveness, and intellectualism. I reflect each day on my life experiences and how they all have contributed in making the composite I call "me." When my father was near death from a progressive neurological disorder, I was unable to be with him in his final days because I needed to be with my son Aaron, in Virginia, for one of several surgeries following his bicycle accident. The last moments I spent with my father involved the most intense connection I ever had with him. His eyes told me he wanted me to stay with him because he was afraid, and he knew he was going to die. His eyes also conveyed the wisdom of his gentle soul that knew I had to be with my twelve-year-old son. His eyes told me I could go, for the sake of our family, for the sake of the next generation, the continuation of our creed. The intensity of those last moments I spent with my father is a significant part of me. I made a decision and because of my father's gentle wisdom, he approved. Thankfully, I was able to tell him I loved him and say goodbye . . . he died within two days of my departure.

YOU—

# ALLOW TIME TO BE YOUR BEST FRIEND

Allow time to become your best friend, not your worst enemy. Do not become a slave to the clock, but a person who enjoys every moment that time offers—for free, with no strings attached.

All your life's experiences happen over time; they do not come rushing to you, all at the same time. Each one can be cherished, enjoyed, and savored. Once you establish your goals, do not expect them to be fulfilled immediately. In reality, all the best things are worth waiting for, no matter how long it takes.

By taking time and allowing experiences to come to you, in time, you become the owner of that experience, and that in itself is a blessing. Without time, there would be no time to savor and be in awe of it all . . . and every moment of time is filled with miraculous awe.

ME—For most of my life, until very recently, I'd always been in an impatient hurry: to get my educational degrees, to get my work done, to get out of traffic, to secure a better job, to get ahead in life, to answer questions. Now as I approach my sixties, I look back and regret all the glorious moments I neglected to savor in my rush to get things done. I am doing my best to make up for it, now. At work I take the time to enjoy all the challenges and personalities. When I take a course or training, I savor the information and the other people with me. In traffic I have manifold choices of listening pleasure: classical music, opera, the Beatles, the Rolling Stones, National Public Radio, books on tape, learning a new language.

YOU—

# ALWAYS TAKE THE TIME TO DEAL

Always take the time to deal with the everyday small problems. This is a good strategy for two reasons: by attending to small challenges, you'll prevent them from growing into large, more difficult challenges. Though you'll spend more time dealing with problems in the short run, you'll avoid having to take more time in the long run.

It's also true that the cost of ignoring the small issues can accumulate and sap your strength. When you face your small challenges one at a time, you'll find yourself able to greet each day with feeling fully charged and full of positive energy. By taking the time to fully attend to even the smallest nagging problem, you will become more effective in dealing with larger issues. You'll have more energy and concentration to focus on all that you want to accomplish.

ME—Since childhood, my favorite way of dealing with conflict and difficult issues was to avoid them and retreat. This is still my choice. At work, however, I have learned the hard way that avoidance breeds infection. When the first lawsuit filed against the agency I direct crossed my desk, I tried to ignore it. The second suit arrived on the heels of another mailing from the first one. I tried to just take it all in stride and ignore all of it. But by the time the fifth lawsuit came, my desk was clogged with paperwork from the first. I began to realize that ignoring these issues wouldn't make them go away. In fact, they only became more complicated and time-consuming. I eventually realized that I saved enormous amounts of time by handling each situation as it arose.

YOU—

# ARE YOU CURSED BY CHANGE?

Do you feel cursed by change? If you do, it may be because you need to change your understanding of change.

Change isn't a curse but a part of living. It's an opportunity to let go of the old and welcome the new. Change allows us to release the past, which will never be again. All that exists is the present, and it is up to us to make the most of it. Change allows us to take the first step into a future we can control by our thoughts and actions. Through change, we arrive at exactly where we want to go.

In fact, those who are really cursed are those who are stuck in their old ways, in their own past histories. Make change your best friend because it will allow you to fulfill your dreams.

ME—As a young adult, I was ill prepared for change. Unready for the responsibilities of adulthood, I clung to some of my childish passive aggressive tendencies. I didn't express how I felt, I dealt with anger through avoidance and retreat, and I gave my spouse the silent treatment. I was, however, very successful overcoming this passive aggressive tendency at work: I gracefully and directly dealt with numerous business and economic cycles, tax changes, legal changes, paradigm changes in the delivery of human services, and government funding changes. I am much better at curbing my passive aggressive tendencies with other people, although I still deal with my anger by "stirring up" others (e.g., bringing up a political issue in social conversation, knowing others will react strenuously). I still work at being connected, in a positive and emotional way, to other people: by concentrating on listening, by doing kind things for others, by showing I care when others are in need, by being generous with my time.

YOU—

# AT THE END OF THE DAY

At the end of the day, how do you feel? Are you tired from just getting through, or are you tired yet feeling satisfied and fulfilled from all the day's fine achievements? There is no better tired than that which comes from a good day filled with accomplishment, after which you are ready for a restorative night's sleep, awakening the next morning energized with positive enthusiasm.

Don't fear growing tired . . . don't measure out your days to save your energy. Instead, live every day fully and plan on ending each day looking forward to a satisfying tiredness. That's how to experience the joy of living and how to glimpse your own potential greatness.

ME—During the times I grappled with clinical depression, fatigue dogged me. During the days when I was symptom free, I almost always felt good about how I spent my time. I enjoy the feeling of being tired that results from a job well done. I have evolved and grown so that I can feel satisfied and fulfilled from most of my interactions with other people. Some days of the month, when I have an evening commitment, such as a Board of Directors meeting or a United Way presentation, I drag myself forward after eight to ten hours of decision-making and meetings to attend another three hours of more work. I drive home tired, but satisfied at the success of the long day. I work hard at accepting the good and the bad and try to recognize that what many people define as bad is really good. I always go out of my way on a bleak, gray, rainy day to comment on how glorious the rain feels and how important it is to life on earth.

YOU—

# AVOIDANCE

Avoidance can be helpful. We need to avoid danger, and to avoid those experiences and people that keep us from the light. Negative *kharma* (invisible spiritual life force) is another good thing to avoid.

Many times, however, we avoid things because we are not in the mood, or just do not want to face a conflict or unpleasant issue. In these cases, we need to avoid avoidance. Putting off what has to be done is never a solution. Facing your obligations and conflicts with sincerity and forthrightness will always spread positive energy to you and everyone else.

You add real value to living when you convince yourself that what needs to be done should be accomplished now, not at some undetermined time in the future. When we put things off, we avoid commitment; we shirk our obligations and promises. If the avoidance bug comes your way, overpower it by thinking about what you need to do next and taking steps to accomplish it. You may need to do this more than once. That's OK. "Now" is always better than "later."

ME—The first time I had to confront a subordinate at work I wanted to hide in my office. But the employee wasn't doing his job, and people at the agency were suffering. And until I confronted this person, I wasn't doing my job. The confrontation was not near as difficult as I had feared, and the monkey was off my back and where it belonged—on the back of the other person. I had done my job and the agency and I were better off for it. I have always favored avoidance and retreat over confrontation, but once I took the first step, it was so satisfying and empowering that I never turned back. Confronting family and friends, relationships in which there is no hierarchical ranking, proved more daunting, but with practice (i.e., rehearsing what I would say so as not to cause undo emotional angst), I have come to liberate my mind and relationships more and more.

YOU—

# BE HELPFUL

Be helpful, not helpless. If there is something that needs to be done, get it done. Don't wait for someone else to do it, or for it to get done by magic. Magic is for entertainment; it does not really exist.

Helping yourself and others will help you lead a better, more joyous, and more fulfilling life. There are numerous ways to be helpful. You can help complete strangers when they inadvertently drop something or need help putting their luggage in an overhead compartment. You can help people you know by simply asking if they need any help, or by just doing something without asking. You will always help yourself whenever you take immediate, thoughtful action in the course of daily living. Be the one to act when you do not feel like it because the payback will always be abundant. Helping is a G-d given gift for each of us to fully enjoy.

ME—As the oldest of two children, I was given free reign to explore and do as I pleased, within limits. My family did not discuss personal or emotional issues unless there was a serious problem, and I learned to live avoiding discussion. I also learned to enjoy retreating to the isolated solace of my room for pleasure and to avoid conflict or meaningful discussion. This learned behavior became my strongest defense mechanism . . . passive aggressiveness. By not confronting or dealing with issues, I didn't help resolve them. By moving away instead of toward others, I was clearly not living fully. To be helpful, I learned, meant being in the show, not in the bleachers. I always found helping strangers, an easy and rewarding past time; saying hello to toll takers, helping someone with a flat tire, giving directions, stowing carry-on bags on airplanes. Helping my family and friends took more effort: listening without judgment to woeful tales, helping move to a new address, calling people for no other reason than to say hello, offering food and shelter.

YOU—

# BE SOMEONE

Be someone who gives to others and you will receive it back many times over. Be someone who cares for others and you will be cared for. Be someone who cherishes friends and you will have many. Be someone who honors others and you will be feted. Be someone who gives love and you will receive love. Be joyful and you will radiate and receive more joy than you can imagine. Be someone who is honest and you will attract integrity. Be someone with a positive attitude and you will sow the seeds of happiness and accomplishment.

ME—In high school I was an outgoing, gregarious, jokester who took great pleasure in finding and talking to the more withdrawn, shy types. My immediate reward for this behavior was the smiles and laughter I was able to evoke. My long-term reward, totally unexpected, comes whenever I pick up my yearbook and read the comments of some of my classmates: "Thank you, Rob, for taking the time to allow me to see how my shyness is not something I need." "I will never forget your silliness and wonderful laugh, especially when you spoke to me!" In spite of my class clown reputation, I grew up somewhat of a loner. I enjoyed my own company. But over time I began to feel isolated. I realized that being alone is fine, as long as it is balanced by a healthy and meaningful interaction with other people. Now, if I spend most of the day at home, I need to get out and be with people, even if it means simply going to the food store. By giving of myself to others through conversation, action, and attitude, I have learned that what I receive in return is much more than I ever imagined or expected.

YOU—

# BE SPECIFIC ABOUT YOUR WANTS

Be specific about what you want and it will be easier to obtain. If you tell a taxi driver to take you to a restaurant, she will not know where you want to go. If you tell a travel agent you want to see South America, she will not know where to book your trip. If you tell your beautician to give you a stylish hairdo, he will not know what to do.

The same applies to your goals in terms of who you want to be and what you want to achieve. Be specific about what you want, and think it through, step by step. Your journey will not only be easier but you will also be more likely to obtain what you wish. We are surrounded by abundance, but we often lack focus. Become clear about what you want, and then reach for it with confidence.

ME—As a child, I never had a clue what I wanted to be when I grew up. Neither my parents nor guidance counselors were much help, leaving me to decide on my own that I'd make a great civil engineer since I loved the outdoors. What I neglected to factor in was the fact that I had no aptitude for engineering. After I was about to fail my first semester at college, I dropped out for a while and then switched to a liberal arts curriculum . . . a good choice for someone as unsure of his goals as I was. An excellent counselor I met during my last year of college guided me toward work in the field of human services. With my goal more in focus, I attended graduate school in this area. Now I don't have a single career regret—and I'm eternally grateful to the man who helped me learn to focus on my goals and strengths.

YOU—

# BE TRUE TO SELF AND OTHERS

Be true to yourself and others by doing what needs to be done. Be true to your family and loved ones. Be true to your community and beliefs. When things go wrong, do not complain and fret; figure out what needs to be done to make things better, and do it. Good people do not believe that the world owes them anything; they simply are thankful to make a positive difference for themselves and the world. Good people make life so much more pleasant for everyone; they protect, feed, entertain, inform, and keep us healthy. Be one of them and enrich life for everyone.

ME—I have always taken pride in being a "what-you-see-is-what-you-get" kind of person. Although there are many things I would have done differently over the course of my life, especially when I view it with 20-20 hindsight, I also know that I did very few things under false pretenses. Sure, there were times when I acted immaturely or inappropriately, but I remain proud of who I am and who I have always been! I never tried to be anyone else or to change my personality to fit the circumstances. I spent much of my youth and early adulthood hiding from my Jewish roots, pretending to be just another American Caucasian male, fitting in with the majority of people I learned and worked with. Once my sons were born I came full circle, acknowledging with pride who I am and where I came from with all its richness, sadness, and beauty. I am a firm believer that being my natural self, with all my gifts and faults, is many times more satisfying than trying to be someone I am not.

YOU—

# BE YOUR OWN PERSON

Be your own pathfinder. You are a unique, special, blessed human being. Why would you want to be like someone else, or pursue another's dream? Your dreams are just that . . . yours alone. Carefully choose your dreams and go after them, in a methodically and purposeful manner.

Your imagination and creative ability will allow you to overcome any obstacle or barrier that might stand in your way. You decide what path to follow, and, if you do not succeed, take another path. There are infinite paths to take to attain your dreams; you just have to be dedicated enough to make the effort.

What you want to take from others are the lessons they learned along their way . . . not their dreams. You can't follow anyone else's particular path to success because it will always be different from yours. By following your own path, you will successfully fulfill your most cherished dreams.

ME—Since my boyhood, there have always been people I respected and admired . . . my parents, my Uncle Irv, my lifelong friend Doug Carver, Willie Mays, Franklin D. Roosevelt . . . but I have never wanted to be anyone else but me. It was not until my fifth decade that I realized this self-respect and self-love was very healthy. I hold no illusion that there is anything unduly special about who I am; it is simply that I really love who I am, and I recognize that we are all very similar, but still individually very unique. Being in love with myself has allowed me to see the good and bad in other people, just as I see both in myself. Recognizing myself in others enhances my efforts to reach out and touch them in a more meaningful way. My only caution, to others, and myself is to not allow self-love to turn into hubris.

YOU—

# BECOME JOYFUL

Become joy by infusing each of your moments with it. Do not wallow in circumstance but create the positive energy needed to improve and overcome adversity and unpleasantness. Wherever you go and whatever you do, feel infused by your big heart, pulsing with joy and happiness. Your joy can transform even the most dire and trying circumstances; you have the power to turn dross into gold, to illuminate the most dreary and dark corners.

Do not wait for joy to come to you: bring it to the world through your own thought, words, demeanor and actions. Whatever the situation . . . good, bad, or in-between . . . keep joy alive and you will really live.

ME—My most endearing memory of joy occurred the day and moment when my depression lifted, when a doctor finally found the best medication suited for my chemistry. I had just left my credit union office and was driving to work when the joy of being alive and the belief that everything would work out rushed through my body, igniting my face with warmth and a huge smile. Suddenly, I noticed the bright sun as it glistened off my car's hood and heard the birds singing joyfully in the trees. Since that moment I am fully cognizant of the critical importance of each moment, and dedicated to making each one count . . . full of happiness and positive energy.

YOU—

# BEING KIND

Being kind makes the world a better place. Kindness gives strength and hope to others, and in turn returns strength and hope to you. A kind gesture is worth a thousand words; a kind act is worth a pot of gold. If you're unkind or avoid being kind, you're choosing a long, uphill battle to happiness, for happiness will never arrive until you start being kind.

Kindness overcomes adversity; it helps heal the wounds of despair, and modulates our feelings of dread. September 11, 2001 was a day of incredible terror, yet we also remember the thousands of people who displayed incredible kindness. When we are kind, we resonate with the universe and bring heartfelt joy to all.

ME—Many of us learn to be kind from our parents, as I did. Aside from a few ridiculous childhood pranks on friends, I cannot remember a deliberate unkind act I have ever committed—though naturally I have my share of unkind thoughts. I love to see the body language and hear the words of those to whom I give my gift of kindness. For example, while in Boston with my son Aaron, I gave a homeless man one dollar, and the heartfelt joy in his thank you and warm smile was worth at least one thousand dollars to me.

YOU—

# BEING PRESENT

Being present allows you to stay focused, and to exist in the present moment, connected with the beauty all around you. Where you are and have always been is right here, now . . . embrace it, love it, flow with it . . . and live. The abundance is yours for the taking, and living in the past or worrying about the future will keep you away from all the richness that is already yours. The venues for being present are numerous: with others by really listening to what they are saying; with nature by appreciating the miracle and wonder of it all; with your own senses by taking pleasure in each moment of taste, smell, sight, sound, and touch; with yourself by enjoying your own company.

ME—I was never really taught how to be present, nor did I learn it easily since I grew up mostly alone in my room at home. In my aloneness I learned to visualize and fantasize. In fact, the only place I felt "present" was in my fantasies. Having a rich fantasy life didn't help my relationships since I didn't know how to stop fantasizing when I was with other people. As a result, I always felt isolated. All through my schooling I remained a poor listener; instead of hearing and responding to the person I was with, my mind would wander. By the time I turned fifty, I learned to become more focused by paying close attention to nature; I'd concentrate on the beauty of the weather, and the beauty of the plants and animal life around me. In time, I was able to listen to people with the same attention that I bestowed on nature. Gradually, I became a much better listener, father, friend, and partner.

YOU—

# BEING UPSET

Being upset usually serves no useful purpose because it can take you away from the determination that success requires. When we're upset, we tend to make foolish and unnecessary mistakes that leave us further rather than closer to our goal. Being upset from an emotionally trying event is natural and healthy; carrying the upset for days or weeks after the emotionally trying event is unhealthy and unnecessary as it serves no useful purpose . . . it only keeps you stuck on the things that have become part of your historical past. Being upset about future events is also needless and unhealthy since your rumination is not useful.

If you encounter obstacles, accept them, live with them, and keep moving toward whatever it is you want, with renewed determination and assuredness.

ME—When I am upset, it goes right to my digestive system. I now know that if I could more quickly express my feelings of anger, I could avoid a lot of time in the bathroom. I have learned, through many years of practice, to let go of being upset for some future event. I was able to accomplish this in a step-by-step fashion: 1. I remind myself that being upset is of no value; 2. I concentrate on not ruminating about what's upsetting me by doing other things; 3. I remind myself of my past experience with the futility of being upset; 4. I reduce the time I devote to being upset; 5. I stop feeling upset.

YOU—

# BLAMING OTHERS

Blaming others is a favorite pastime of many people. Affixing blame and fault is a good way to insure you remain static; you're stubbornly stuck in the past tense, and the past will not help you enjoy the present.

Blame-fixers are almost always part of the problem because they rarely, if ever, admit they were to blame and if they were, they will never reveal it. They may convince themselves that the carping, blaming person they have become is who they want to be. Do not fall into the blame-fixers' trap. Devote your energy to finding and following the best choices you have and creating the best future that you can envision. By living now and moving forward, you become part of the solution, not part of the problem.

ME—Though I never considered myself a blaming person, I fell into the trap of blaming my ex-wife for the breakup of our marriage. In other words, I became part of the problem, not part of the solution. Now I can acknowledge that we were both at fault, but at the time, I was just as intent on blaming her as she was on blaming me. The more bitter we grew, the more stuck and intractable we each became. Looking back, I wish one of us could have called a halt to the blame game so that we could have more quickly moved forward with our new lives.

YOU—

# BOUNCING BACK

Bouncing back is a critical and essential life skill. When horrific and negative things happen, we need to move quickly and forward, as opposed to freezing and moving backward.

In disaster and crisis, never allow your shock to paralyze you. Being resilient . . . bouncing back with a positive purpose . . . will keep you alive in a meaningful way. It does not come without effort and sacrifice, but in the end you will live beyond your fears and become the best you can be. When in doubt, remember the millions of people before you who overcame great challenges and obstacles: Thomas Edison, Ann Frank, Mahatma Gandhi, Opray Winfrey, Ellie Weisel.

ME—After a truck hit my son . . . he was only 12 . . . I encountered a very deep and heartfelt sorrow that over the years evolved to a full-blown clinical depression. Frozen in time by the extent and seriousness of my son's injuries, I was only able to tend to his immediate medical needs. As for my own serious emotional needs, I neglected them. In fact, I denied them. I did not bounce back emotionally for many years, and this had a negative effect on me and everyone around me: my family, friends, and co-workers. Now I realize that I was unable to bounce back in a healthy way, which would have entailed getting the attention that I needed, so I could once again become the effective person I was always meant to be.

YOU—

# BREATHE IN AND OUT

Breathe in and breathe out . . . and you will, with effort and concentration, learn to be present and live the moment. By feeling the peaceful serenity of simply being, you enable yourself to clear and calm your mind. By concentrating on the breath, with practice, you can let go of negative thoughts, let go of judgments, and enjoy the pure pleasure of now.

Keep the past as something very far away and the future as something you know nothing about. Focus on accepting the experience of the present moment and fill it with your positive energy. You can start practicing in many ways . . . by quietly sitting, exercising, competing, painting, or participating in a hobby, conversation, or group activity. By getting in touch with all the serene moments that are always available, you will realize positive possibilities for living.

ME—I learned about yoga and *pranyama*, or the energy of the breath, after my divorce. I found the quiet solitude of the non-judgmental yoga class exactly what I needed to help me through my struggle with worry, sorrow, and increasing mental illness. It was uncomfortable at first, sitting on the floor, my aching leg muscles unaccustomed to the various *asanas*, or yoga postures, such as 'Easy Pose' or 'Lotus Position.' Once my leg muscles adapted, I began counting each breath, and gradually I was able to clear my mind from the clutter of thoughts. In this way, I found some relief from my deep psychic pain. It's was not a panacea. But with discipline, I was able to generalize my practiced serenity throughout the day until it became a part of who I am.

YOU—

# BRING ALL YOUR POTENTIAL TO LIFE

Bring all your potential to life. Dig deep to assess your true nature and your hidden, or understated potentials, gifts and strengths. Bring them to the surface to use them in your quest for connectiveness and self-actualization. Open up your gifts to others, use your strengths to improve your life, hone your potentials into useful tools. Once your potential surfaces, you will have no reason for doubt, or insecurity. You will be empowered to be all that you want to be.

You can't know how much you can do and how far you can go until you take the first step. Move forward with persistence and courage to scale the tallest mountain, work through any obstacle, and reach any goal. It is with these tools that your best possibilities are brought to life.

ME—It was only after I began to meditate on a daily basis that I was able to gain clarity about my *"kundra"* (center) and my perception of my true nature. At first, the negatives or dark side of my nature caused me a great deal of uneasiness, but with time I was able to accept my dark side that was more than balanced by my light. The negative feelings that I had about myself—that I was self centered, selfish, an egghead, cheap, disconnected, without feeling, a non-reactor, a space cowboy, a jokester, immature, and dependent—began to seamlessly merge with the part of me that was generous, witty, a crowd pleaser, patient, funny, good natured, genuine, honest, forthright, intelligent, bright, caring, confident, sophisticated, down-to-earth, tranquil, and a decision maker. Taken together, all these traits add up to my true potential.

YOU—

# BRING OUT THE BEST IN OTHERS

Bring out the best in others by being who you really are. If you want to impress people, don't strut your own stuff, but work on showing them their very own best qualities. Empower them to touch their real selves.

The best engineers do not complete all the work on a project themselves; instead, they position themselves as a critical, contributing part of a team that collectively solves problems. The best salespeople do not force themselves on others; they guide their customers to see what they really need and want. The best teachers are not the ones who possess the most knowledge, but those who inspire their students to want to learn on their own. The most impressive people are always the ones who are able to bring out the best in others.

ME—During my teenage years, I had no idea who I was or who anybody else was. And I was not particularly interested in finding out simply because I perceived myself to be a happy young man leading a full life. As time went by, I began to realize more and more the critical importance of not only knowing who I was but also of gaining some insight into others. When I became Executive Director of a large nonprofit organization, I quickly learned that my success was very closely allied to the success of all those who worked for me because without them I was powerless. I learned that I could empower others simply by allowing them to do their job and giving them honest and forthright praise and criticism. On the social front, I was always able to amuse people and make them laugh, but friendships only became meaningful and worthwhile when I was able to bridge the gap between I and thou, that is, when I was able to take an interest and understand what others need, want, and desire . . . which many times was directly opposite to what I wanted or liked.

YOU—

# CHALLENGES

Life is challenge and how you live life depends on how you view and accept challenge. If you run away from all challenge, your life will be one of retreat and non-involvement. If you take on all your challenges in a resentful spirit, you miss all the pleasure of accomplishment and success. If you accept and welcome all your challenges with gusto and excitement, then your life will be filled with gusto and excitement.

Challenges exist to give us the opportunity to make a choice, to move us forward in wisdom and knowledge, to insure we cherish living. As we work through challenges, we are able to tackle more and more of whatever life has to offer, and become more appreciative of all the unchallenging wonder around us.

Even if you have failed at some challenge in the past, use your disappointment to propel you forward by transforming that disappointment into a positive force for success. Past failures are simply present opportunities, and all opportunities have built-in potential . . . this time, you just may succeed. If you have had many disappointments, then your life is filled to the breaking point with opportunity waiting for you. Complaining and whining about all your disappointments only increases their power to influence your present life. Leave all your disappointments where they belong . . . in your past . . .

and start working with renewed excitement, energy and resolve to succeed. What are you waiting for?

ME—When I chose engineering as my college major, even though I had no real interest in or talent for the field, I did so poorly that I had to leave school just before Thanksgiving. At first the challenge was frightening; I felt stigmatized by my peers as a dropout, and uncertain if I could succeed at college when I returned. With the support and encouragement of my parents, I quickly pulled it together, and returned to school as a liberal arts major the very next semester. I was not overly gifted in school but because I took classes I really enjoyed, attending school became pleasurable. My status as a dropout soon became a historical event that propelled me onward . . . eventually, to four degrees.

YOU—

# CHOOSE TO CHANGE

Choose to change today, not tomorrow. Commit to rid yourself of those old wishes, worries and concerns that keep you stagnant. Your simple act of conscious commitment is the first step; next, make a concerted effort to terminate your old worries and concerns. Rise above all the distractions and destructive habits that keep you down and locked in "nowheresville."

It does not happen right away, but with time and proactive effort, you can choose to change. This frees you to move forward with zest and determination to achieve everything you always wanted. With positive determination, rejoice in the abundance of possibilities you have, to overcome all that keeps you static, and to persevere through every challenge.

Be mindful, though, that "Rome was not built in a day." Your wishes do not materialize overnight; they become reality through your dedicated incremental effort . . . one step at a time.

ME—At periodic intervals in my life I find myself thinking I am in "nowheresville." It usually comes whenever there is a slow down in my activity level or after the completion of a project, like the writing of this book. The lesson, I have learned is to allow the feeling and accept it. After a day or so, I commit myself to exit "nowheresville" and find a new interest or project. The simple thought of finding something of interest is very uplifting because it takes effort and I am engaged in its positive outcome. Once I settle on something the thrill of anticipation slowly builds as I take all the action necessary to achieve my objective. It certainly does not happen overnight but I have found it to be my engine for living, an active thoughtful mind and dedicated effort toward a goal.

YOU—

# COMMITMENT

Commitment is the first step to change. Right now, in this very moment, if you commit to making your life joyful and happy, it will begin to happen. It starts with your honest and heartfelt promise to do so. Once committed, then you begin to establish the plan that you will follow each moment of each day.

The plan needs to involve both the thinking, feeling, and doing realms. You need to think through what you want, feel comfortable with the thought, and begin taking action to achieve what is most appealing and fitting for you. Part of this commitment involves ridding your mind of negative energy and harmful thoughts that do nothing to help you. You need to commit to actively doing things that will bring you closer to your goals. You need to make a plan to stick with, for your own sake . . . after all, this is your life, not anyone else's.

ME—After my divorce I found myself unsure of who I was. Once I committed myself to change, I had to think through and feel what was most comfortable to me. My goal was to discover who I was and what I wanted from life. I established a plan to explore things I enjoyed doing. The plan was wonderful because it involved daily activities just for me. Over the course of two years I discovered many things I enjoyed but the real adventure was discovering not only the things I enjoyed but who, at my heart of hearts was I. What I found was who I always was . . . a happy jovial person who enjoyed others and cherished time alone. Thanks to my commitment I started to live my life more fully, in total acceptance of who I was and what I enjoyed.

YOU—

# COMPREHENSION

Comprehension, another gift we all share, is our means to understanding the world in all its diversity. Appreciate this gift and your life will be filled with meaningful, glorious experiences.

The more you open your mind, the more you will be able to comprehend other people, appreciate their points of view, and the more powerful, prosperous, knowledgeable, and effective you will become. With an open mind, you will become aware of the beautiful diversity of acquaintances and friendships surrounding you . . . and you will make more friends. Appreciation of diversity is not just acceptance of those who look and act differently than you; it is appreciation of others who think and have opinions different than yours.

A closed mind limits knowledge and understanding. We end up surrounded by those who think and feel as we do. Close your mind and you will lock yourself in a self-conceived prison. You'll think of yourself as a victim, and experience yourself as a prisoner of your own mind. A willingness to comprehend others, however, is the key out of that prison.

ME—When I first moved to New York City to start my career, a sheltered, naïve, middle-class suburban boy from Westfield, NJ, I was shocked and appalled at the incredible diversity of human life I encountered there. My job... tracking down and bringing to treatment those with active and potentially active cases of gonorrhea and syphilis... brought me face to face with people of every race, creed, religion, and sexual orientation. I faced corruption and purity on a daily basis. To do my job, I had to rely on my powers of comprehension. By better understanding the people I worked with, I knew I'd be able to treat them with more respect. I ended up feeling dazzled by all I learned about the complexity of human life.

YOU—

# CONFLICT

Conflict, an unavoidable part of life, can be the spice of life. You can allow it to defeat you or make you a more whole, appreciative human being. Avoiding conflict is in the same realm as avoiding life.

One of the joys of living is the resolution of conflict, not its avoidance. Conflict resolution requires compromise, and compromise requires a willingness on your part to let go . . . of prejudice, fear, worry, and anxiety. This doesn't come easily; it requires effort. But what you gain in return will be well worth it. The rewards of resolving conflict go beyond merely overcoming another challenge: you are part of a solution rather than part of a problem; you are proactive rather than reactive; you are feeling rather than passive; and most importantly, you are alive, making a statement, and living life as it was meant to be lived.

Let go of avoiding conflict; you will find you will become more enlightened, more connected, and more pleased with who you are.

ME—I grew up in a household in which none of us raised our voices or argued, at least openly. As a result, I never learned about conflict or its resolution. Instead, I learned, as I mentioned, to become passive-aggressive; that is, I expressed my anger vicariously, raising issues that caused others to react assertively, aggressively, and/or passionately while assiduously avoiding any conflict that involved myself directly. I didn't deal with this deficiency until I turned fifty. The conflict I had avoided for nearly fifteen years of a twenty-five year marriage was divorce. Once my wife and I separated, the toxicity of our relationship became apparent, and the eventual divorce resolved the conflict and emboldened me not to avoid future conflicts.

YOU—

# CONTINUAL MOVEMENT

Continual movement is essential to living. In life, our bodies move, our minds think, our hearts pump, and our blood flows. When movement stops, life stops. Think of being helpful in terms of movement. Movement is part of living. Helplessness is characterized by a lack of movement. Carried to the extreme, the absolute lack of movement is how we define death. Life, however, is full of choices, and making choices involves movement. Choosing to move and to help will bring you great satisfaction and joy.

To take advantage of all of life's miraculous gifts, we have to keep moving. When you wake up, don't spend too much time in bed anticipating what kind of day you might have: get up and get going. When you arrive at work, think about your day's agenda and begin to work on its success. When you finish your workday, change gears and start thinking of your familial, social, recreational, or relaxation needs. When you get home or to your planned destination, start doing what you had planned in a welcoming way.

ME—As a child in a libertarian family, I was given full reign to play hard and have fun. Always active, I enjoyed jumping, running, climbing and swimming. My interest in sports propelled me to keep moving, and playing. As I grew, this need to stay active motivated me to take on new tasks, try new things, and succeed. When the blood and tissue in our bodies stop moving . . . we are dead. When we stop moving . . . stop going on, we begin the process of dying. No matter how dark the circumstances are, and to me, mine were very dark, we must always find the strength to get out of bed and keep moving . . . keep living. When I became clinically depressed, I stopped moving. I found a way out of my depression through yoga—a system of patterned movements, and psychotropic medication. For me, keeping moving is one of life's secrets. I don't worry about succeeding or failing; I just try to stay in motion. Medical science has proven that when we are actively moving about, chemical endorphins are released in our brains that make us feel good.

YOU—

# CRITICISM

Criticism can be the same as avoidance. When we use our time to criticize others, or complain about our fate, we are succeeding at avoiding the treasure of living. Real living involves people who take action, do things, move, help, and are part of the solution, not part of the problem. Complainers are most often part of the problem; they need the leadership and example of a person who pitches in to make things better, get things done. You can be that leader. Complaining and doing nothing does not bring out all the things life has to offer because it becomes a very unfulfilling, difficult way to live. Are you in the arena of living, or are you in the bleachers watching it all happen, criticizing what you see on the field? Get out of the stands and get into the game of life.

ME—While writing this book, I spent a week at the Green Gulch Buddhist Farm in Sausalito, California with my life-long friend Doug Carver. We agreed to help support the Farm by working four hours a day as part of our meditative experience. One day, I was assigned, with two other much younger men, to manually cut down forty-foot high bamboo trees with small hand-held saws. After the first hour, the physical labor in the hot sun was quite intense, and I decided to move to a more secluded section of the grove. One may think that I moved in order to stop sawing and take a nap, but in fact, what I did was find a way to continue to saw as I rested on my belly. By finding a creative way to keep working, while not carping about how hot and difficult the work was, I was able to stay active and complete the task. Helping to load the downed trees onto the truck at the end of the day, and recognizing my contribution to this effort, will remain one of my sweetest memories.

YOU—

# CURIOSITY AND EXPLORATION

Curiosity and exploration make the world go round. When you are curious and explore new experiences or pursue answers to questions that interest you, you add value to your life and others. The effort to find answers that arise from your innate curiosity makes the world move forward in a positive, life enhancing way. When you explore, you enhance your confidence and self-assuredness by learning new things, meeting new people, and experiencing new perspectives.

What are you curious about? What makes you wonder? What makes you want to explore? Now is the time to start exploring and open up a universe that has always been waiting for you.

ME—I've always been curious about things that give me pleasure and satisfaction. As a child, I was curious about activities that brought attention to me and impressed my peers: learning how to hit a home run, learning how to be silly, learning what makes others laugh. As an adult, I learned that curiosity about people, places, and things also brought me new pleasures and satisfaction. By talking to others about the things that interested me, I piqued their interest; they valued my experience. As I satisfied my curiosity by exploring history, opera, art, yoga, meditation, religion, and spiritualism, I shared my explorations with others, possibly enhancing their lives.

YOU—

# DESIRES

Desires can be understood if you dig beneath the surface to find out what it is that truly fulfills you and gives you peace, tranquility and joy. Most often, you'll discover not material things at the root of your desire, but the more sensual things that you may have forgotten or lost . . . the natural joy of the bright sun, the radiance of a rainbow, the warm sense of another's love, the sweet sound of the birds, the soft touch of baby's skin, the taste of cold watermelon on a warm day, the textured feel of corn on the cob.

Once you have uncovered your desires, analyze them and dig even deeper to understand their underlying meaning. When you achieve this understanding and know what you truly want, go for it. You already have the capacity to fulfill your true desires for love, passion, sensing, knowing, understanding, and exploring.

ME—I grew up with plenty to eat and always enjoyed the sensation of taste and filling up. As I aged and became less active, my joy of food and filling up began to show in an ever-expanding waistline. After my seventh diet, and dealing with the health-related issues of obesity, I realized through the help of Jean and my own digging that what I was doing was filling up emptiness and loneliness. Like worry, eating had also become my best friend. My awareness is helping me significantly to keep my weight down, but I know that the struggle is life long.

I was fortunate to have parents who did not covet possessions and lived frugally. When I was married, I owned automobiles, houses, furnishings, and valuables. I have come to realize that all the things I once accumulated owned me more than I owned them. The cars I purchased for my wife and sons needed maintenance and insurance. My home required constant upkeep: yard work, painting, repair, and renovation. My furnishings and valuables constantly wore out and needed replacing or repair. Yet I was very attached to all these possessions and afraid of losing them, a fear that was rooted in my past. Now my desires are totally liberated from possessing and I am much more interested in cherishing life. Every moment of every day I take enormous pleasure in the simple gifts of my senses and nature.

YOU—

# DISSATISFACTION

Dissatisfaction need not be negative. When you are dissatisfied with something, you have the unique opportunity to transform your dissatisfaction into satisfaction. Think of it as a challenge.

If something you want seems to be beyond your reach, do not despair; nothing is beyond your reach and nothing is impossible. All you need is a determined plan and concerted effort. When you are dissatisfied with someone or something, bring your mental and emotional gifts to the challenge and devise a plan to become satisfied. Where there is a will, there is always a way, and you will be empowered in the process of discovering that path.

ME—When my relationship with my wife became toxic for both of us, our separation and divorce was a wonderful opportunity for each of us as individuals to create a more joyous existence for ourselves . . . to turn a dissatisfying marriage into satisfying futures.

Whenever I was dissatisfied with the behavior of board members at BARC I carefully mapped out strategies to deal with my dissatisfaction. I learned over and over again that patience was always the best policy since aberrant personalities are usually their own worst enemies. On one occasion that lasted for several years, I was up against a very savvy and experienced corporate senior manager. He mounted a fierce campaign to discredit both the agency and me, causing me much dissatisfaction, to say the least. He came close to orchestrating my termination, but in the end, his own twisted *kharma* failed and my intense dissatisfaction turned around, as I became friendlier with him.

YOU—

# DO NOT ALLOW DOUBT

Do not allow doubt to stand in your way. Doubt can discourage you from achieving your goals. Whenever you doubt your ability to do something, you begin to not achieve it. Whenever you allow doubt to become an important part of who you are, you insure that your dreams will always remain just that . . dreams.

The best way to overcome and eliminate doubt is to walk away from it with a small baby step. Then, take a slightly bigger step, and yet a bigger one, until you are completely convinced that there is nothing you cannot do if you put your mind to it. Start with something small. If you doubt your ability to cook, for example, first make a spaghetti dinner. Next time, graduate to lasagna, and then move on to something even more demanding. Keep your cooking self-confidence in memory as you take on more and more challenging issues, like making a speech, or running for public office.

ME—I've never been plagued by doubt . . . except when it comes to my musical ability. I love to listen to music but cannot carry a tune and seem to be tone deaf. This didn't bother me much; in fact, I enjoyed playing the trumpet. But in first grade, a crotchety band teacher said to me, "If you keep playing your trumpet like that, Schram, I will make you scram!" After this threat, I pretended to play for the rest of the class and never returned. Doubt had entered my world. Years passed and a much kinder, gentler, young eighth-grade music teacher heard me singing off-key. Instead of embarrassing me in front of the chorus, he asked me to stay after class and worked with me for a few minutes. He then encouraged me to continue singing . . . but softly. His good mentoring helped erase the sting of doubt I'd lived with.

YOU—

# DO THE THINGS THAT GIVE JOY

Do the things that give you joy. Whenever you are annoyed or frustrated, simply ask yourself if what you're annoyed about will still matter one year from now. If your answer is no, then how important can it really be?

When you focus on small frustrations, you miss all the wonderful opportunities to enjoy the great aspects of life that are available to you . . . for free. If you enjoy yourself right now, in this moment, it will always remain with you as a warm, fond, memory. Enjoying this moment will remind you that you did not miss all that is important in your life. You will also have no regrets. When you focus on what matters most, you add value to your life and the world around you.

ME—The first lawsuit I experienced at BARC was devastating. The local plaintiff attorney, who previously worked for the local newspaper, began to leak unsavory details of the case, for all to read daily. At the time, I was unaware of the question, "Will this matter one year from now?" I now know that it did not matter even one month hence. By allowing things that happened at work, or in my social life, to ruin my day and linger with me in the form of worry, I allowed myself to miss the abundance of goodness and pleasure available to me. I cannot easily remember the people and the things that annoyed me in the past, but I certainly do recall the richness of things that continue to give me pleasure.

YOU—

# DON'T SWEAT THE SMALL STUFF

Don't sweat the small stuff . . . and, as author Richard Carlson reminds us, it is all small stuff. Think about all the little things that bother you: waiting in line, buying a car, slobs, inconsiderate people, silly people, stubborn people, rainy days. Now, think of all the big things that bother you: work, war, your boss, and your spouse. Regardless of which column your worries appear in, the point is that they are all small issues in the face of the plentiful abundance available for you to appreciate every moment of every day. Once you open yourself to living each moment, all your bothers become small stuff. What problems on your list can compete with the beauty of a rainbow? What can compete with the joy of doing a good deed? With the love you have for your children?

When you commit yourself to making every moment count, you relegate all your annoyances to the status of "small stuff"—where they belong.

ME—Like many people, I prioritized my issues into big and small stuff and by so doing I lived many years absent the appreciation for all the abundance available to me. In my younger years I consumed myself with the problems of the world and making money, and missed all the gifts of simply breathing and being alive. It was only in my sixth decade that I truly understood why it is all "small stuff." I didn't devalue world problems; I simply realized they are not part of my existence or something I had power over, and when I dwelled on them, I was allowing myself to focus on issues other than myself. We can't ignore all the challenges in our lives. Divorce, marriage, unemployment must all be addressed. But as we address these, we shouldn't lose sight of the gifts of living.

YOU—

# EACH MOMENT IS AN OPPORTUNITY

Each moment brings opportunity to live. How you live depends on how you experience each moment. When people say hurtful things, it is your response that determines how much they hurt, not the words themselves. When the opinions of others hurt you, it is your response that determines how much they hurt, not the opinions themselves. Difficult times are only as difficult as your response to the difficulty.

The quality of your life depends on how you live each moment and react to external stimuli. How you choose to think, feel and act determines the quality of your life. Other people and all the environmental externalities have nothing to do with your happiness. Your happiness is totally dependent on how you experience each moment and all that is external to you. In other words, the quality of your life is entirely up to you. Live the unique and miraculous life you were blessed with.

ME—I have never been overly sensitive to criticism or hurtful comments by other people, but I have allowed difficult times . . . such as my son's accident and my failed marriage . . . to weigh me down. My perception of my son's accident and the never-ending surgeries and rehabilitation for his injured arm was devastating, especially when his mother blamed me. I allowed my guilt to weigh heavy on my heart and I began to walk through each moment of each day as if I weighed 900 pounds. Thanks to a gifted surgeon in Virginia and Aaron's incredible ability to move on with his life, my perceived heaviness began to lighten. I allowed this heaviness to overwhelm me again, when I confronted my failed and toxic marriage. It was only when I separated from Shirley knowing that Aaron and Justin were independent college students, that I finally improved the quality of my life and began to live the life that was always available. With hindsight, I now know that my guilt-ridden response to these difficult times was absolutely unnecessary. By my response to these events, I cheated myself out of many more happy and fulfilling years.

YOU—

# EACH MOMENT . . . NOT TO BE SQUANDERED

Each moment brings you closer to death; however, you may have many moments left. Since you do not know when your time will come, isn't it a good idea to make the most of all the moments you have?

Time has molded you into who you are, and will continue to forge your dynamic persona. Isn't it in your best interest to fill those moments with meaning, joy, and passion? The clock of your life stops ticking only after your heart stops. No matter how many moments you may have squandered until now, it is never too late to correct the balance. It is always up to you to make this moment, this day, this week, this month, this year, better than the last, or better than it has ever been. In your time, the more good you give and experience, the richer your life will be. Then, when your time comes, you will continue your soul's journey without any regret.

ME—When I turned fifty, I realized that I had more years behind me than ahead of me. This realization was painful, but it also helped me in my journey toward daily joy and fulfillment. I began to realize all of my blessings: my sons Aaron and Justin who completed their educations and are happy, well adjusted, and gainfully employed in their chosen professions; my partner Jean whose intuitive insight and love have given me much solace and guidance; the spirits of my parents who are within me always; my sister Lynne and her husband Ralph and their sweet children Shawn and Alison; my close, life-long friend Doug; my many social friends; my education; my religious and spiritual understanding; my rather significant ego; my financial security; my physical and mental health; my extremely rewarding career at BARC where I have been able to achieve all that I ever dreamt about accomplishing; my joy of being alive!

YOU—

# EFFORT PAYS

Effort does not cost; it pays. The time and resources you invest always bring a reward. Many of us shy away from putting forth an effort when it's required, but this is shortsighted of us. When effort is sincere and focused, it always has value. Effort teaches and trains you for living. It strengthens you and helps you grow.

Do not expect your effort to necessarily payoff immediately; often, it will take time and sometimes it will have an impact in unexpected ways. But no matter how or when it appears, a payoff is behind every effort.

ME—In my forties, I decided to run in the New York Marathon. Though I'd never before run in a marathon, I was trim and fit, and couldn't wait. Training each day in the streets and parks of Piscataway, NJ, my senses were so enhanced that I could tell how long cars on the roadside were parked by the smell and feel of their emitted heat. I had visions of my hunter/gathering ancestors running down the tribe's dinner and becoming part of the landscape. My breath awareness was most acute; I was able to detect any undesirable particles in the atmosphere and felt incredibly appreciative of clean air loaded with the oxygenated life force. One day I completed seventeen miles, my longest onetime jog, along the Raritan River. But that run, my longest, took a severe toll: I suffered dehydration, near delirium, and bleeding nipples (from tee-shirt rubbing . . . a somewhat rare but not unknown condition for marathoners). Stumbling home, I collapsed on my bed in a state of exhilarated exhaustion. I never did run in the marathon, but that period of training left me with a feeling of accomplishment that will always be with me. In fact, my effort to train for the marathon made running in the actual race insignificant because I was able to derive such profound pleasure from the preparation alone.

YOU—

# EVERY MOMENT IS GOOD

Every moment is filled with good wonderful things happening all over the world. The sun shines brightly giving warmth and sustenance. The rain cultivates and sustains. Every moment has a past that just ended, and that is why it is counter-productive and sheer folly to live in the past or be guided by what was. Embrace this moment, love it, breathe it, feel it. The past is finished; the future doesn't yet exist. To dwell on either of these is to lose precious present moments. There is only right now, and you can always move forward, if you desire. What is holding you back? It is never too late to start, because the past just now ended.

ME—"Taking time to smell the roses" is a very powerful mantra. It means that every moment of every day is a miracle for us to enjoy. During my years of attending to my career and raising a family, I often lost sight of this miracle, but fortunately for me, I have rediscovered it. Driving to and from work, I take a moment to appreciate cloud formations, the sound of rain, my car's tightly engineered steering. When I leave my car, I breathe in deeply to appreciate the smell of the air and its surrounding environs. I love the give-and-take of being in the presence of others . . . appreciating my gifts to them and their gifts to me. I live my appreciation every moment of every day.

YOU—

# EVERYTHING YOU DO MATTERS

Everything you do and think matters because it impacts on other people, the world, and the universe. In the grand scheme of things, all living things are connected to each other. Think of what happens when a tiny pebble is thrown in a pond . . . the ripples extend everywhere.

Negative thoughts generate twisted *kharma* (invisible spiritual life force) which cause suffering and unhappiness. But by filling our minds with positive thoughts, we radiate wonderful *kharma*. By filling our actions with love and kindness, we fill the world with joy and happiness. You are a unique and important part of the universe . . . what you think and do reverberates on the greater whole.

ME—Each day, at work, I try to repel twisted *kharma* by thinking positive thoughts that produce a clear, shining light. On overcast, cloudy, rainy days I breathe in the freshness of the air, feel the cool rain on my face, and listen to the gentle sound of its pitter-patter on the roof. The rain sooths my spirit, ensures life, and keeps a smile on my face. I particularly enjoy telling people I greet that it is a "beautiful rainy day!" I can see how much they appreciate my efforts to turn a potential negative into a positive.

YOU—

# EVERYTHING YOU NEED YOU HAVE

Everything you need, you already have. Your natural way of existing is one of joy and pleasure, not worry, dread, and fear. Surrender to your insecurities and start this moment to enjoy the pleasure that you have always had. Joy is not something that takes time; it is all around you, waiting for you to recognize and embrace it. Joy has no price, no cost. It just is! Joy comes to you when you release yourself from all your negative and destructive habits. Joy has nothing to do with your life circumstances or how you perceive those circumstances; it has everything to do with how you really are and how you really want to be.

ME—Although I have always lived a relatively Spartan life style, I have never felt poor or deprived. The absolute beauty of my life style shone most brightly after I lost all possessions through divorce. Each day I was able to more fully appreciate all that living offers. Once I freed myself from insecurity, worry and attachments, I became more connected to all that had always been around me. I derive great pleasure from sitting in my favorite chair and really listening to music or watching some local sparrows feed their young hatchlings.

YOU—

# EXERCISE CONTROL OVER ACTIONS

Exercise control over your actions and avoid the activities that are not right for you. When you have an inner conflict, allow your enlightened, experienced side to win. Whenever you are able to perceive your feelings about an issue, you are above the issue, and in control of deciding what you need to do. Suppose you're tempted to exact revenge against someone who has hurt you. Instead of letting hatred into your heart, take a step back and rise above the feeling. Logically and gently take control and move forward in a positive, life-enhancing way. Inner conflict is most difficult whenever you are immersed in it. You will be able to resolve conflicts much more easily when you rise above them rather than sinking into them.

ME—When I was in the seventh grade at Edison Junior High School in Westfield, NJ, my friends and I walked home from school each day past the house were a boy named Tomar lived. Tomar had mental retardation and would inevitably be mowing his lawn in a peculiar way . . . he walked with a very stiff back . . . and my friends and I would mock him by chanting his name as we walked past his house, "Tomar, Tomar, Tomar, Tomar . . ." Tomar was always fixated on his chore and I doubt that he ever heard us over the drone of the lawnmower, but I'm sure his parents did. I knew what we were doing was wrong, but I couldn't seize control of my actions and suggest to my friends that we stop. Twenty years later, when I was appointed Executive Director of BARC, an agency supporting people with mental retardation in the community, I thought of Tomar. In the intervening years, I had learned how to take control of a situation so that it didn't cause pain . . . but I wished I had learned this lesson years earlier so that my efforts could have helped Tomar and his family.

YOU—

# FACING YOUR FEARS

Facing your fears allows them to evaporate. Ignoring your fears allows them to fester, intensify and rupture elsewhere. Running and hiding from your fears empowers them and allows them to dictate your happiness. Acknowledging your fears is the first step in facing them and ridding yourself of their negative influence.

Every step you take in facing your fears shrinks them accordingly. The effort you expend to face your fears weakens them proportionately. Likewise, this effort strengthens you, and brings you closer to who you are. Fears can vanish; strengths endure.

ME—Though I was often the class clown, I'd grow incredibly anxious whenever I had to give a serious public presentation such as a speech. My palms would sweat, my heart would palpitate, and I feared I would forget the words. Needless to say, I never volunteered for speaking parts. In college, I began to face this fear by taking an elective course in public speaking. The speeches I was obligated to prepare and deliver did not ease my anxiety but I learned the important techniques of public speaking and began to learn to manage my anxiety. After college, I took jobs that required public speaking . . . to groups of volunteers and service clubs. Each time I spoke, I felt a little drop of fear drained out of me. After thirty years of practice, the sweaty palms and heart palpitations are 95% gone. As to the remaining 5%, I use it to my advantage: it helps me maintain my edge, and reminds me to engage with the audience.

YOU—

# FAILURE IS HELPFUL

Failure is helpful for progress. When you fail, you create a myriad of opportunities to succeed. Failure simply instructs us that a particular strategy does not work and need not be tried again.

Whenever you meet obstacles or challenges, do not despair. Instead, see them for what they truly are: opportunities to succeed and achieve your goals. Life is always presenting us with multiple paths; when one leads to a dead end, take another one rather than stagnate. The answer to the question, "Will I succeed?" should always be, "Yes!" because it is all a matter of will, determination, and positive outlook. Failure should always be viewed as an opportunity to succeed.

ME—I failed at having good manners as a child. I failed at making the high school basketball team. I failed at being an outstanding student in high school. I failed at having a steady girlfriend in high school. I failed at studying engineering after one semester of college. I failed at being a good friend. I failed at being a good husband. I failed and was fired from several jobs. I failed at being the best father I could be all the time. Without my failures, I would never have obtained my considerable successes . . . four college degrees, a wonderful job, a wonderful partner, two beautiful sons, and daily unquestionable appreciation for living.

YOU—

# FEEL GOOD AND MAKE GOOD

Feel good and make good. If you want to be the best that you can be, it begins with you. You and you alone need to make the difference by feeling good and making the world a better place.

We all have a choice: is our outlook gloomy, filled with wonder and joy, or somewhere in between? Choose the wonder and joy, and your life will dramatically change for the better. You have an abundance of gifts and a wealth of potential. Strive to be the best you can be and remember that it begins with how you feel. Spread the goodness of joy and love everywhere you go and always act on your inspired feelings of positive possibilities.

ME—Like so many others, I spent many years blaming externalities for my unhappiness. If my wife was not so impossible, I would be happy. If my job paid more, I could feel more secure. If winter was not so dark, I would enjoy it more. If my father was not so disabled, I would not worry so much. My outlook in my first fifty years bounced between gloomy and joyful depending on the circumstance. I needed to realize that my circumstances were just that, circumstances . . . and not the guideposts for my feelings. That's when my liberation began.

YOU—

# FEELING IS NOT WHO YOU ARE

Feeling is not who you are. Who you are is deep within you, at your core. Some people never find who they really are and become how they feel, at any given moment. People who are more fully evolved make the effort to find who they are, in the deepest recesses of their soul, and live a life filled with the abundance that is everywhere.

The first step toward self-actualization begins the moment you decide to find who you truly are. You are capable of controlling your mind, your body, and certainly your thoughts; you simply have to practice and make the effort. You will not be transformed overnight, but with focused effort, you will get closer and closer to who you really are, and what you can really achieve and do. It may sound like magic but it isn't: you just need to realize that you are who you have always been. If you think you are your job title, your position in the family (mother, father, brother, sister), your degrees, your achievements, or your wealth, then you are missing out on the much more important aspects of your being. You are a unique, special creation, and there are no others like you. You are an integral, connected part of the universe and what you do and how you act affects the entire universe. What could be more exciting than taking the first step and finding out who you really are!

ME—I spent all of my married life defining who I was by my titles . . . son, father, brother, husband, executive director . . . and very little if any time defining and doing what was important and meaningful to me. It was only after I was divorced and my sons left home that I began to realize just who I was and what I wanted. Coming to grips with some of my realizations took some time. I realized, for example, that I was, at times, an egotist, selfish, unfeeling, cheapskate, a loner, and a disconnected space cadet. Coming to grips with some other realizations took no time at all: I knew I was kind, gentle, social, humorous, a good conversationalist, intellectual, playful, fun-loving, dependable, honest, and forthright. With my supportive and loving partner, Jean, I was able, for the first time in many years, to start concentrating on what I wanted for myself. The journey of discovery was most pleasing. I discovered I love many things.

YOU—

# FOCUS ON SELF

Focus on being better than yourself, not other people. Competing against others leads to resentment. Bettering ourselves leads to joy and fulfillment.

Put the energy you use to compete with others into improving yourself. Energy expended to have the best car, the best house, or the highest salary does not improve who you are. Energy expended to help others, love yourself, love others, and appreciate the miracle of nature improves who you are. We are each unique, beautiful creatures who have the capacity to achieve way beyond our dreams. You only have to apply energy to bettering who you are and you will become the person you always were meant to be.

ME—When I was appointed Executive Director of BARC, I was a competitive thirty-one-year old, anxious to achieve and grow the agency. My arrogant, self-confident entrepreneurship was offensive to many human service professionals. I was competing to become the leader of the biggest and most powerful nonprofit agency in Bucks County and the Commonwealth of Pennsylvania. As a member of the Pennsylvania Association of Resources for People with Mental Retardation (an association of human service agencies serving people with developmental disabilities), I met many CEO peers much wiser and experienced than me. I slowly learned over the years that being the biggest and most powerful was not the name of the game. Caring, loving, and doing for others was what human service work was all about. I started to invest energy not in entrepreneurship but in self-improvement. I allowed my arrogance to fade away. By focusing on me, I became a better person, and BARC was one of many beneficiaries.

YOU—

# FOCUSING ON THE POSITIVE

Focusing on the positive is so powerful that all the negative things become minor things that are of no consequence. When you focus on all the good to be accomplished, any distractions become insignificant or nonexistent. Create value and meaning in everything you do and eliminate needless worry that accomplishes nothing. By letting your positive vision pull you forward, you move out of the gloomy realm of worry and frustration and into the bright and most satisfying venue of enlightened engagement.

ME—For years I neglected to accentuate the positive in my work. I focused on all the things that could go wrong: lawsuits, funding reductions, negative press, skyrocketing costs, dissatisfied staff, dissatisfied Board of Directors. My journey through life's ups and downs has taught me the value of focusing on the positive and how it can make all the issues of living so much more satisfying. Lawsuits may come but they have no long-term impact on the health of the agency. Funding reductions and skyrocketing costs may occur, but back-up planning will always help us cope with budgetary shortfalls. The press will print ten positive human-interest stories for every negative one. The number of satisfied staff and board always outnumbers the dissatisfied. My experience has shown that the old adage, "You can please all the people some of the time and some of the people all of the time, but not all of the people all of the time," is true time and time again.

YOU—

# FOLLOW THROUGH

Follow-through is always critical to fulfillment of your dreams. First, of course, you have to dream, have visions, formulate goals, and set your priorities. But after this step, it's essential to act on them by following through. If you don't, your dreams will become a burdensome weight that only exists on your wish list, and you'll devote your energy to thinking of what could be instead of doing what you want to do.

Of course, it's easier to sit at home and imagine success than to get off the couch and take the first step. Sometimes, we avoid follow-through because we think of all that has to be done. That can be paralyzing. Instead, think of the first thing you have to do. When that step is accomplished, then think of the next. This is one way to train yourself to become a person who follows through on wishes and dreams.

ME—After my divorce, I was somewhat of a lost soul because I only had myself to focus on. What did I enjoy? What did I want to do with my free time? What would I do when I retired? I spent most of my time in the early days following the divorce thinking, dreaming, wondering, and wishing. I couldn't seem to take the first step. It was my partner Jean who awakened me to just how lost I was. With my sons grown, my ex-wife taken care of, and BARC succeeding in its mission to serve and advocate for people with developmental disabilities, I found that my old definitions of who I was were not working anymore: father, breadwinner, husband, executive director. It was only when I started to explore the things that I enjoyed, that I began to really define myself, and begin to follow through on what I wanted. All the things I had envisioned and thought about became an important part of my life.

YOU—

# FOLLOW YOUR DREAMS

Follow your dreams and you will greet each day with enthusiastic energy. Let your dreams pull you forward in a positive, joyful way. The process of fulfilling your dreams is the key; it alone will make your life full and worth living regardless of whether or not your dreams are ever fulfilled. That's because no matter how realistic or unrealistic your dreams are, the act of committing yourself to doing something is enough. Many people have dreams of winning the lottery, but how many of us take pleasure and appreciate the joy of just going to the store, deciding on what lottery number(s) you want, talking to the clerk and other people, purchasing the ticket, and looking around the store for other things you might need? Dreams do not have to be fulfilled to bring joy and pleasure.

ME—I have always dreamed of being a world leader although I have never really desired to live with my personal life fully exposed in the press. I have always known this dream to be an unrealistic fantasy, not only because of the public exposure, but also because I loathe public self-aggrandizement, a requirement of national or international leadership. In analyzing this thirty-year old dream, I realize that what I really want is to be recognized. Not only have I followed this dream in its more realistic form by becoming an executive director, but also I continue to follow it in my second career as a teacher and trainer.

YOU—

# FOR EVERY ACT OF VIOLENCE

For every act of violence, there are thousands of acts of human kindness. We read and hear about acts of violence and hatred taking place everywhere in the world, and it is easy to allow this bad news to obfuscate all the wonderful and kind acts that occur every moment of every day.

Whenever someone is in need, there is always some kind soul to help. Whenever there is a job to be done, there is always someone ready to step forward and help get it done. Whenever there is a tragedy, there are always people who go out of their way to assist. There is never a shortage of kind, gentle, and helping people. Out of every need, out of every job that has to get done, out of every tragedy comes the absolute beauty of human kindness with its clarion call that life is a priceless gift without compare. Open your life to the goodness all around you.

ME—I see acts of human kindness from the time I get up in the morning until I go to sleep at night. Whenever there is an accident on the road, people always stop to help. Whenever I am short-staffed at BARC, people always step forward to help. Whenever I travel, people are always available to help me find my way; they even offer food and shelter. I no longer watch the news on television because of its overwhelming emphasis on negative, twisted *kharma*; all I see are people hurting other people, fires, and natural disasters. I much prefer to watch my neighbor cut the lawn of our elderly neighbor or teach his children how to ride their bicycles.

YOU—

# GENUINE HAPPINESS

Genuine happiness comes to those who seek and want it. It takes dedication and effort in order to search out the genuine. Sometimes the search begins with the realization that many seemingly happy moments are in fact transitory. An increase in pay is soon forgotten after we receive the first paycheck. A child's joy playing with a new toy often diminishes after the first time.

Genuine happiness is not something material or something that you wait for; it is something that is available to everyone, all the time. It does not need to be found or understood; it simply needs to be chosen and appreciated. No matter what your life circumstances are, happiness is available to you. Choose it and live it.

ME—One of the reasons I find genuine happiness in nature is because nature isn't transitory: it's a constant in my life. The seasons always come and go, the waves always pound the shore, and rivers always flow to the sea. The love I now have in my life . . . for my partner and for my grown sons . . . also has the ring of permanence; it's not something that comes and goes. I can also count on the genuine pleasure I take in being with others as something unchanging in my life. Through these constants, I have found genuine happiness.

YOU—

# GIVING THE EXTRA EFFORT

Giving extra effort, going the extra mile, is a good idea. Success almost always results from giving an extra push rather than stopping your effort or falling behind. For example, if you set aside an hour a week in which to embark on a project you've always wanted to begin, that's fifty-two newfound hours each year, enough time to read the books you've been meaning to get to, to learn French, or to write the first draft of a book you've long been incubating.

Putting forth extra effort in this way accumulates exponentially over time, and makes your chances of success much more likely. Whenever you are tempted to walk away from a task without giving it your all, make a conscious decision to reverse course and invest a little more time and effort. You will not be disappointed at the results.

ME—Without making an extra effort, I would have remained a college dropout. Without extra effort, I would have become a chronic job drifter. Without extra effort, my agency, BARC, would have gone out of business. Without extra effort on the part of my wife Shirley and myself, our sons would have grown up aimlessly. Without extra effort, I would have lived out my life ignorant of who I really am and what I want.

YOU—

# GOING WITH WHAT WORKS

Going with what works is a simple idea but is so often ignored or overlooked. Your own experience is the best guide for what works best; it's much more reliable than doing what you think is expected of you or following the popular fad.

Because we're each unique, we each have our own way of working. Some of us need to show up at our desk every day at the same time. Others wait for inspiration to strike. Some work best alone; others, as a member of a creative team. What's important is finding what's best for you.

Finding what works may not happen right away. Thomas Alva Edison, for instance, failed hundreds of times before he discovered a light bulb that worked. Yet he stuck with his plan until he succeeded.

Effort and failure make success more valuable since you put in so much time to find it. Discovering how you work is as much a part of the process as making your way to your goal. Identify what methods work for you, and then go with it.

ME—Because I had no first-hand experience of what it felt like to be married, I relied on the marital relationship I knew best . . . that of my parents. Theirs was a "until death do us part" relationship. I never thought to consult other people. If I had, I might have discovered that there are many different types of successful marriages, and that the goal is to find the type that works for you. Instead of trying to go with what would work best for me as a married man, I clung to my parents' version of marriage . . . and ended up divorced to boot. I'm not sure if my sons would have been better off if my wife and I had divorced years earlier than we did, but I am sure that I would have been better off.

YOU—

# GOOD LISTENING

Good listening will always be rewarded in kind. People need to know they are being heard; sometimes, that's *all* they need. Being a good listener shows people you care. You need not always have an answer; you simply need to be present, to be there, with another person. A good ear is often worth a thousand words of advice. When you listen with care, attentiveness, knowledge and compassion, you not only connect to another person, but you also help heal the entire world.

Always use your ears before engaging your mouth. When you really listen, your words are forged during your concentrated attention to the words you hear. The most effective communication is always a two-way process during which good listeners forge words for each other.

ME—As a rambunctious teenager who always wanted to be heard, good listening was an alien concept to me. As an egotistical, assertive adult, good listening remained alien. I was the kind of person who always wanted to have answers, and truly believed that my answers were as good as anyone else's. But eventually I had to acknowledge that my poor listening skills had become an increasing liability for me in my work, with family, friends, and even with my wife and children. During one of my many mid-life crises, I realized that I had to work at improving my listening skills. Because I'd become quite adept at mind-traveling when I was supposed to be listening, I found the challenge to become a good listener very daunting. I worked hard to stay focused, especially when listening to boring renditions of things that held little interest for me. I've improved, but I still have work to do—especially since I know that caring takes many forms but listening is one of the more powerful ones.

YOU—

# GRATITUDE

Gratitude... what a wonderful and powerful feeling! Be thankful more than you are thankless. Try not to take anything for granted. We're so used to overlooking many of the basic aspects of our life that should inspire gratitude. After all, many more things in life go right than go wrong. The miracle of breathing goes right, for example, as long as you are alive. For the miracles of seeing, hearing, touching, feeling, tasting, loving, knowing, and communicating we should always feel grateful.

We all succumb, at times, to the virus of ingratitude. We worry that we haven't gotten enough, or any at all. We dwell on what we don't have and become embittered. Feeling grateful, thankful, for what we do have releases us from the narrow prison of ingratitude. Giving thanks, whether silently or aloud, is always a healthy activity.

ME—During my most difficult times . . . Aaron's accident, my wife's alcoholism, my unhappy marriage . . . I found it hard to feel grateful. That didn't feel strange at the time; after all, how could I feel grateful about my son's serious injury? But now that gratitude has come into my heart, I realized that I missed an opportunity years ago. Instead of withdrawing, as I did at the time, as a means of coping with my pain, I could have focused on what I was thankful for. Even in the darkest times, we can feel gratitude in our hearts. If I'd been able to feel grateful for what I had . . . a healthy body, a family, the changing seasons, a curious mind, the help and support of friends and family . . . I may not have fallen into a depression. With my most difficult times hopefully behind me, I am even more appreciative of all the miracles I possess. My gratitude is so deep that everyday I do my best to share it with others.

YOU—

# HABITS

Habits do not have to dominate your life. There is no rule that says conflict has to make you feel stressed, or a rainy day has to make you feel sad. You are not obligated to continue any habit, especially negative, nonproductive ones. The next time you find yourself reacting to a situation as you habitually do, stop yourself. Ask yourself if this is truly how you feel, or if you are reacting without really thinking. The rain doesn't have to make you feel blue; focus, instead, on how cozy it feels to be indoors on a gray day. The next time you find yourself in an argument with someone and start to feel anxious, think of the argument as a dance: you take one verbal step, and then the other person goes. You could end up enjoying disagreeing. Use the moments you tend to react out of habit into opportunities to learn about yourself and to grow stronger.

ME—Though I have overcome many of my negative life-long habits . . . excessive worrying, passive aggression, for example . . . I still habitually overeat. I eat as a substitute for feeling connected with other people, and for expressing my feelings. I eat when I am happy, sad, stressed, joyous, or for no particular reason at all, except for the pleasure of taste and filling up. Writing this book has helped me to address the emptiness that overeating fulfills. Now, instead of heading for the kitchen when I feel a gnawing, empty feeling inside me, I head for my computer.

YOU—

# HAPPINESS IS ALREADY YOURS

Happiness is already yours; you do not need to struggle and fight for it. Happiness will not be found in great wealth or possessions; these don't satisfy us in any deep way. Conditional happiness depends on something else to happen . . . it is transitory; it doesn't last. Genuine happiness is already yours for the claiming. You simply have to recognize it. You don't even have to go looking for it because you already have it . . . within. And you don't have to worry about losing it.

Happiness needs to flow out from you. If, instead, your goal is to have happiness flow into you . . . if you're looking for the world to give you happiness . . . then you will never know it. Look within. Allow the happiness you discover there to radiate from you. The world needs it, and is waiting.

ME—Happiness has always been with me. I just did not always realize or appreciate it. Today I glow with my happiness. I do not allow conditions or my environment to determine my happiness. I never have a bad day because I truly believe that every day is a gift to be cherished. Life's challenges, of course, do occur, and I view them as opportunities to achieve and shine. The big event in my life that turned me on to the importance of my own happiness was my fiftieth birthday, and knowing that I had fewer years ahead of me than I had behind me. Just being alive is wonderful enough. The beauty of nature and other people is a very precious bonus.

YOU—

# HOW YOU USE YOUR TIME

How you use your time will determine how you live. Is your life static? Are you a couch potato who dreams of accomplishment? Are you a spectator viewing life from the bleachers? Or is your life filled with motion, thoughts, words, and actions that give you pride, joy, and satisfaction? We live for a finite amount of time; it's only logical that we use our precious time to our own best advantage. Entertaining negative and self-defeating thoughts and behavior is a waste of time; it will not bring about the kind of life that you deserve. Changing your life to one of beauty and meaning is up to you, not anyone else.

ME—With my family grown and living independently, I have a lot of time to decide how to use my time. I appreciate all of my accomplishments in education, work, and family but I do not rest my case, my life, on the past; to do so would be to give up on life, and I am all about living and enjoying. With achievements in work, education and family behind me, I have developed new goals to pursue and enjoy. I am committed to journey throughout the world, at least annually, to see and experience things for the first time. I am committed to writing and publishing. I commit a lot of time to watching with awe, professional basketball, and playing golf.

YOU—

# IMAGINATION

Imagination is limitless. It's also vital. Without imagination, we wouldn't be driving in cars, flying in airplanes, reading by electric light, or logging on to our computers. Everywhere we look around us, we see the fruits of someone's imagination.

We all have the capacity to imagine; we're born with it. But some of us know how to use it and how to get lost in it, while others need help. Our imagination allows us to dream, to plan, to enjoy flights of fancy, or to just indulge ourselves. Imagine yourself connected to it all, full of positive energy and motivated to seek whatever it is you desire. Now take this imagined image and begin to think of all the steps you need to take to make it happen. Then start by taking the first step and every step thereafter, one at a time. You will find that everything you imagine has distinct possibilities for achievement. Imagination isn't just child's play. It's for all of us throughout our lives.

ME—As a child and young adult, I always imagined myself in charge of things. What began as a grandiose fantasy, was tempered over the years. Today, I realize that my childhood imagination has come true . . . I have helped thousands of families over the years in my role as executive director of an agency. When I think of it as an evolution, I see how useful and powerful my imagination was. Today, my imagination is always with me. I imagine myself in various positive realms of existence (as an explorer, rabbi, sage, teacher) and have fun playing out various dramas in these created realms. Although, I know my current use of imagination is fantasy, I also realize that it has elements of reality; I take adventure tours throughout the world at least once each year. My interest in Judaism is growing daily. My knowledge of religion, its practice and universal connectedness, grows with each passing day. I do a significant amount of teaching and training.

YOU—

# IMPROVING

Improving on what is takes away any need to worry about what was. You can always improve on what exists now . . . so, forget about what was; you cannot change history. Learn your lessons from the past, but do not live in the past . . . it is over. You are blessed with the ability to improve and the opportunity to do so is right at your fingertips . . . it is simply up to you to take it. You can make your life one that is always improving the good and the bad things that you experience. Life will always have ups and downs . . . it is up to you to go with the flow and make it better for the future.

ME—Self-confidence has always been helpful in allowing me to take all my failures in stride and move forward. Once I stopped worrying about things I had to deal with (travel arrangements, a long drive, buying for birthdays, a BARC lawsuit, the weather, etc.), I was able to more effectively work on improving. I met a fifty-five year old female resident of the Buddhist Green Gulch Farm in Sausalito, CA who spoke to me, in detail, about the birth of her twenty-five year old daughter, and the successful, wealthy people she had met at the farm. From listening to her, I realized that she was someone who lives joyously, in the past. I was flabbergasted at the incredible joy and heartfelt love she expressed, not at how her daughter is now, but how perfect and miraculous her birth was twenty-five years ago . . . as if it had happened yesterday. She was a woman who clearly was not working on improving the present or making plans for the future . . . she was just someone who was existing on her past joy, and not fully relishing the now. I am very pleased at my past wonderful moments, but I am even more pleased that the joy I get from present wonderful moments is one hundred times more pleasure-filled, simply because it is happening now, and I am fully experiencing it in the present moment.

YOU—

# IT IS A WIN-WIN SITUATION

It is a win-win situation every time you do not have to be right, every time you compromise in order to build or maintain a relationship with someone else, every time you put your energy into understanding another point of view.

Cooperation and understanding are far more powerful than always knowing and being right. Always being right creates isolation whereas understanding and cooperation create integration and connection with others. Being part of the larger whole, rather than a segregated, errant piece, is what living is all about. Are you trying to win at life or are you trying to live?

ME—The relationship in which I was the least compromising was with my wife, Shirley, and our marriage took on a lose-lose dynamic culminating in our divorce. The arena in which I am most likely to compromise is work. Not surprisingly, my work relationships . . . with the Board of Directors, the parents of children with disabilities, and my staff . . . can be characterized as win-win. With Shirley, I was convinced that I was right and she was wrong, and we ended up apart. The "truth" as I perceived it was more important than our marriage. At work, I willingly listen to others, and state my opinions, however forcefully, in the appropriate context and at the right times. Working together to help the families and people we support is my most important goal. The relationship endures.

YOU—

# IT IS ALL ABOUT THE PROCESS

It is all about the process, not the destination. When you want something, develop your plan, and then go into action. But remember that your destination is only half of the reward. The journey itself counts for the other half.

To just focus on where you're going is to close your eyes to all that's available to you as you make your way. In the process of reaching your destination, you have challenges to overcome, people to meet, places to go, and things to do; all of these challenges are the fabric of what makes life so interesting, so much fun, so joyful. Rather than always thinking ahead, concentrate on what you're doing now and take pleasure in it.

Some goals may be more challenging to achieve than others, but the process always will take your disciplined focus and effort. You may find yourself at a different destination than you envisioned. You may even find that the pleasure you take in the journey exceeds the pleasure upon arriving.

ME—When I played semi-professional baseball in Westfield, NJ, I won the league batting title. But what I remember best about that season isn't the award, but the thrill of competition I encountered at every game, particularly the last game of the season in which I had four hits in four at bats. The journey, in other words, trumped the title. The same is true in another very different arena. I thought I couldn't get any happier than I was on the days each of my sons were born. But in truth, watching them grow into the fine young men they are has exceeded my happiness at their birth.

YOU—

# KNOW YOURSELF

It is possible to hide your thoughts, feelings, and actions from others, but they are never hidden from the person you really are. In your heart of hearts, you always know who you really are. You can't hide from yourself.

Embrace who you are . . . your good points as well as those aspects of yourself you'd like to change. Changing begins with acknowledgement and acceptance. You can only become who you really are through effort and by taking action that will move you toward who you have always been. By your actions, you give yourself reason to be proud of who you are, not embarrassed or ashamed. Make a commitment to be real and make yourself proud.

ME—I spent many years disconnected to my feelings; in a very real sense, I didn't know who I was. Connecting to my feelings after decades of disconnection did not come easily, but the process was essential. I used a chart of "feeling faces" to help me identify familiar feelings (exhausted, confused, guilty, suspicious, hurt, confident, mischievous, happy embarrassed, depressed, cautious, ashamed, lonely, hopeful, in love, jealous, bored, surprised, anxious) and unfamiliar feelings (ecstatic, angry, hysterical, frightened, smug, enraged, overwhelmed, shy). By reintroducing myself to me, I allowed myself to fall in love with myself. By loving my true self, I became empowered to connect more with others. Now I can enjoy the dual pleasures of being alone and of being with other people.

YOU—

# KEEP AN OPEN MIND

Keep an open mind and you'll be amazed at what you will discover. You'll learn things about people you never knew; you'll understand the world in a whole new way.

So often, we approach others with our biases firmly intact. When we listen with bias, we hear only what we want to hear, not what is actually said. It's a way of shutting out the world, and never changing.

Our growth as people depends on living with an open mind.

ME—My poor listening skills for most of my life were a manifestation of a closed mind. I approached the people in my life as if I knew everything about them before they even opened their mouths. I'd pigeonhole them, and then listen for only those comments that reinforced my impression of them. I was able to open my mind through living with my soul mate, Jean. Jean had spent many years in therapy learning about herself, and how the world perceived her. Jean had what I considered initially to be an annoying habit; she would complain to me whenever she sensed I was not really listening. On occasion she would test her sense by asking me what she had just said. Many times, to my embarrassment, I was unable to tell her. I began to realize what my wife and sons had been telling me for years; I was a poor listener! Acknowledging the truth about myself was only the first step in opening my mind. The more difficult work was changing what I had been doing for fifty years. By constant practice and concentration, my mind opened, my listening skills improved, and I am a better person.

YOU—

# LEARN FROM FAILURE

Learn from failure and move forward. Everything worth achieving takes effort, and part of that effort entails accepting failure. Anything worth achieving does not come easy, which means you probably will fail at some point in your life.

If you do not learn from your failure, you are destined to repeat it. Analyze and learn all that there is to know about why you failed, and then you can move forward with confidence that you won't repeat the same mistake. That doesn't mean you'll never fail again. But even multiple failures are not cause for despair. Think of them as gifts that make the ultimate achievement of your goal all the more satisfying. If everything you wanted was served to you on a silver platter, your satisfaction would be very low, if not non-existent. Only that which we must work hard for brings satisfaction. Today's failure may well be tomorrow's success.

ME—If I never learned from my failure of opening one group home, I never would have been able to open up thirty group homes. With the first group home, I allowed the township's solicitor to invoke an illegal exclusionary township ordinance in violation of the Federal Fair Housing Act. I nailed the failure coffin shut by allowing an attorney who was a former board member to represent the agency in our hearing with the township. He was ill prepared and we lost. Failing is the greatest learning aphrodisiac, dwarfing all other methods of teaching.

YOU—

# LET PERSISTENCE GUIDE YOU

Let persistence guide you. If you do not succeed at a particular endeavor, make sure you give yourself time to experience your disappointment. But when that feeling passes, as feelings always do when we give vent to them, begin to make plans to try, try again. You may have to do this more than once to attain what you want, but it's always the right strategy.

When you persist, even in the face of failure, you give yourself opportunity to analyze what went wrong, and to remove that option as a possibility. The more possibilities you remove, the closer you come to your goal. You may be tempted to give up, but that will leave you with nothing. Persistence leaves you with the promise of one day succeeding.

ME—As a nonprofit executive, I knew that funding diversity would insure program continuation because all the proverbial eggs would come from different baskets. When I first came to BARC, we were a one-source funded organization. I faced a number of obstacles in developing more funding diversity: board resistance, staff resistance, Bucks County office resistance, and parental resistance. The various resistances provided for many disappointments but in the long term, my persistence paid off. Slowly but surely, over many years, we diversified our funding into the private sector, the federal sector, other counties, and other state agencies. During fiscally trying times we found that when one or more of our funding sources were cutting back, others were growing. My persistence resulted in BARC being able to continue all its programs and expand over three decades.

YOU—

# LETTING GO OF EGO

Letting go of ego is the first step to finding yourself. That's because your ego is the biggest barrier to finding ultimate peace and joy. By letting go of self and ego, you will experience much more connection with the world around you. You won't need your defense mechanisms.

Ego is like a filter through which we see the world in terms of "I." By letting go of self, we come into relationship with what really is. Close your eyes and free your mind of all thoughts . . . let go of self . . . drift into nothingness . . . and slowly come in contact with reality. Float with it; do not question it. You are a part of the world, not the entire world. Let go of your ego, and find the world

ME—I grew up with a very large, well-developed ego. It was through yoga and meditation that I learned to let go. In yoga, my first letting go of my ego occurred during a full week of yoga training at the largest yoga ashram in the United States . . . Kripalu in Lenox, MA. On the third day, I suddenly realized that my body motion was flowing with my breath effortlessly, and I was thoughtless . . . a true epiphany of being in the now. Letting go of my ego through meditation, or just sitting, took several years of dedicated practice. I started by simply counting each breath in and out to one hundred and then starting over again . . . and again. Slowly my thoughts began to diminish and eventually I was thoughtless . . . just breathing, just being. By just being I truly felt how connected I was to everything. My ego and mind simply became manifestations of my soul in a breathing vehicle—my body.

YOU—

# LIFE IS A SERIES

Life is a series of ups and downs. By making the best of your life when circumstances are good, you create positive energy and memories for yourself and the world. When circumstances become difficult, you can still make the best of your life by focusing on overcoming obstacles, drawing on positive memories, and persevering. Sometimes it helps to anticipate the difficult times. After all, the only constant in our lives is change. Nothing lasts forever.

Though we often tend toward inertia when we're feeling low, the bad times can be just as educational as good times, if not more so. Whether up or down, we learn about living, about being, about moving ahead, and appreciation for it all.

ME—My life has had its share of success and failure, of ups and downs, of good times and bad times. During my successful good times, I created a great deal of positive energy and memories for a lifetime. Unfortunately, during my failed bad times, the only positive energy I created was surviving through it all. However, I realize that living through it was a tremendous learning experience . . . something to be remembered for any future obstacles I may have to resolve. I successfully lived through my bad times without resorting to drugs and alcohol to dull the pain. The knowledge and wisdom I hold today is a direct consequence of many up and down experiences over many decades. Without my ups and downs, I would be very ill equipped to face all the new challenges that come my way each day.

YOU—

# LIFE REQUIRES ADAPTATION

Life requires adaptation. Whenever you come to an obstacle in your life's path, begin thinking and planning for how to accept it and move on. It may involve adapting to another path, or it may involve staying on your path and adapting to find a way through or around the obstacle. If it is a mountain, learn to climb. If it is an ocean, learn to swim or navigate. If it is another language, learn it. The gift of adaptation allows you to always move forward, regardless of the obstacle in your path. Adapting to the challenges that life provides allows us to use our G-d-given tools.

ME—My life has been full of adaptations. I adapted to my deep fear of getting on a school bus and going to kindergarten every day with the help of my mother who walked me to the bus each morning and just as assuredly greeted me as I got off the bus in the afternoon. Although I did not even know what the word adaptation meant at age five, over time, I felt my rigid fear of something new and dreadful begin to soften. Throughout my life I have learned, through experience, to soften my rigid positions on people and things.

YOU—

# LIVE A WORRY FREE LIFE

Live a worry free life. When you analyze your worry, you will find it needless since it is usually about things you cannot control anyway: someone's illness, the weather, how people will perceive you. Value does not emanate from worry; anxiety and fear emanate from worry. Why not stop worrying and just be?

Begin by transforming your worry into some positive action. If you are worried about your speech to the Kiwanis Club, read it over one more time, and then begin doing something positive, like cleaning the refrigerator or mowing the lawn. If you are still worrying about the speech at bedtime, think about how clean the refrigerator is and how manicured and beautiful the lawn looks. You will awaken refreshed, renewed, and confident. And after the speech goes well, remember how glorious you felt. Hang on to this memory . . . preserve it . . . and use it the next time you feel yourself beginning to fall into the pit of needless worry.

ME—I inherited my love of worry from my father, who was a Class A worrier. My father even looked forward to future worries, telling me, "When you have small children, you have small problems but when you have older children, you have big problems." I took worry on as a security blanket, something under which I kept my disconnected feelings safely hidden so I didn't need to feel them. My recovery from being addicted to worry took time. First, I had to recognize that my worry had a genetic component . . . I inherited it from my father. Next, I realized that I had been denying my flight from connection by retreating into worry. The third step was to remind myself each time I started to worry that it resolved nothing: all it did was occupy my thoughts. The fourth and most difficult step was to say goodbye to worry each time it said hello. As time went on, I became more and more able to let go of my best friend, although he was very persistent and hung on for several years. The fifth step involved taking positive action each time I worried and then letting my worry go. For example, when a member of my board tried to have me fired, I promptly prepared everything he asked for, thus refuting his case. In other words, I turned my worry into action.

YOU—

# LIVE BEFORE YOU DIE

Live each day as if it were your last because it may very well be your last day. Life gives us no guarantees. No one really knows how he or she will think when they are at death's doorstep.

Whether we accept death or fight it, the one thing that makes it easier is to know that you have lived. Go for what you want and live each day to the fullest. After birth, the only absolute certainty is our death. By acting on what you want while living, you can fulfill it during your lifetime. The past is history and the future is yet to be and unknown, but right now is here and will never be again. Live it, love it, enjoy it, treasure it, and be thankful for it . . . for, in reality, it is really all you have. Greet each day with awe and urgency and you will never have any regrets when your time comes to move on.

ME—I have had the privilege of being with many of my closest relatives before they died; they all intuitively knew their time had come. My mother, who had a major heart attack, was in the hospital for bypass surgery. She knew she was not coming out alive, and I sensed she was ready to die. I told her I loved her and we hugged for the last time. My father, who was progressively ill in a nursing home with a neurological disorder, did not want to die. After one of my visits, he wanted me to stay but knew I had to go to Virginia for one of Aaron's operations . . . we exchanged our last "I love you," and I clearly saw the apprehension in his eyes. My Uncle Irv, my childhood role model, a real "*mensch*," was going out to dinner with my parents for his birthday. I sensed something was different about him when he came to me. He had come to say goodbye but could not find the words to describe his feelings of love. My two grandmothers, who both reached their $90^{th}$ birthday, died without communication, as they slipped into unconsciousness weeks before they finally succumbed. My cousin Sylvia died of colon cancer; when we visited, she spoke nothing about herself or her limited time. She was interested, right up to the end, in what new and exciting things our family was doing. The one very critical thing I know is that when my time comes, I do not want to have any regrets about the time I spent living. I work every moment of every day on insuring that I live as fully as I can.

YOU—

# LIVE LIFE SINCERELY

Live life sincerely by being who you are. We each know deep inside when we are being genuine and when we are faking it. If you want to make a difference in your life and create real value, you need to be true to who you are.

Often, we're under pressure to live as if we were playing a game of charades. We worry about impressing others. We become distracted by what others think of us. But these factors aren't significant. We have to be true to ourselves. Look into your heart and speak and act according to what you find there. Be sincere, and others will react to you with sincerity as well.

ME—I try to be the same person, no matter where I am. I don't change who I am according to my circumstances. That doesn't mean I'm not polite. I learned manners the hard way . . . digging into my food before others were served taught me to wait until everyone is served and ready to eat. But I don't worry about being polite when it comes to my core beliefs, or when I am challenged to perform. I do not act differently at home, work, or when I am out socially. I do not spend needless time preparing for how I should act or worry about how other people may expect me to act.

YOU—

# LIVING LIFE IS UP TO YOU

Living life is up to you. What you accomplish each day . . . each hour . . . is up to you and no one else. What choices will you make?

In life, you will meet good, bad and indifferent people, people who want to help you, people who will praise you, people who want to hurt you, people who will criticize you, and the vast majority of people who are indifferent to you. The way you respond to people is up to you. Your choice will determine the type of life you live. Will it be one filled with joy and pleasure, one filled with suffering and pain, or one that straddles both extremes?

ME—The most critical change I made in my life came with the realization and understanding that what is external to me ... people, places, events ... do not dictate who I am or determine my state of happiness. I alone determine my destiny and state of mind. A sobering but helpful realization I had was that if I were to drop dead tomorrow, life would go on as if nothing happened. My sons, my partner, my sister, some friends, and some folks from work would attend my funeral. The agency I direct would continue to function because no one is indispensable. Jean, my sons, and my sister will have no major problem continuing their lives though I hope they will occasionally remember me. Knowing the futility of thinking "I am important" makes living each day fully even more important!

YOU—

# LIVING A POSITIVE LIFE

Living a positive life imbues each moment with meaning and value. The value of each moment may be hidden or overwhelmingly obvious. Appreciating every moment is part of living positively; you live to fulfill each moment without judgment or rancor.

Put a positive light on even the most negative circumstance. This approach does not mean you are wildly idealistic or naïve; rather, it means that you are a pragmatic realist who believes that you have the capacity to change the world for the better.

ME—In 1993, my aunt Catherine, 76, a lifetime smoker, was in the hospital with lung cancer. The doctors had done all they could for her; there was no hope. Shirley and I went to visit her with dread. How could I comfort a dying person? What should I say? Everything about her situation seemed full of nothing but despair. And when I first walked into her room, I felt despairing. She was extremely grateful to see us and was concerned that we not stay too long because we had things to do and a life to get on with. She, on the other hand, was waiting to die. After we had spent more time with her than she desired, she said, in exasperation, "What does it take to expire, anyhow?" Her frankness so surprised me that I laughed; she did not, she was "dead" serious. Here she was, taking the reality of her death by the horns. She was ready to die, and her unexpected courage touched me. She expired the next day. Her final gift to me was realizing that even in the most difficult circumstances it's possible to see a positive.

YOU—

# LOVE LASTS

Love lasts longer than hate. Make love the most important part of your life by living each moment in joy and gratitude. Whenever you feel hatred and anger, quell it with love and understanding. Hate always has a short life and can be overwhelmed with love and peace; it just takes effort and commitment on your part.

Disagreements and arguments are opportunities to show tolerance and understanding, not to become angry, annoyed and revengeful. It is inconceivable that people would want and desire to live in the dark and gloomy side of life when the light and joyous side is always nearby. You have the power to choose: choose the joyous side.

ME—As someone who has always had difficulty understanding and expressing my anger, it has been easy for me to accept peacefulness and love over hate. It's always been easy for me to tell who is genuinely loving and who is angry, even if the anger is well-hidden. Because I'm a gentle soul, I have, on numerous occasions, been able to facilitate calm in some rather rancorous situations, particularly at work. Once, the county commissioners, who oversee a large portion of BARC's funding chose a poor candidate for an administrative job. This person turned out to be disastrous, threatening the livelihoods of many people with whom she came into contact. As a result, the agencies under her aegis turned positively mutinous. The person received threatening prank phone calls, and claimed that her cat disappeared under mysterious circumstances. While others acted out their anger in these ways, I counseled for patience and political intervention if necessary. In the end, my cooler temper prevailed: the county commissioners terminated the administrator's employment.

YOU—

# MAKE A PRESCRIPTION

Make a prescription for success. You can have anything you want. You've been developing your skills since childhood. As a baby, you learned that crying got you fed or changed. As a child, you learned that crying got you attention. You learned that you were rewarded when you did what your parents wanted, that playing with your friends was pleasant, and that stomping in mud puddles was fun.

As an adult, you are well practiced in getting what you want. The issue is first deciding what it is that you desire. Your wish must be specific: don't just wish for a car; make it a blue Mercedes Benz 330. Then, ask yourself why you want this particular car. Is it to impress everyone with your success? If so, then you may conclude that your real desire is to be respected by others.

But it may well be that you desire the car because it is so exceedingly well engineered and gives you great pleasure every time you drive it. You love how it hugs the road, the sound of its acceleration, and it's ease of handling. In this case, the Mercedes may very well be exactly what you want.

Whatever your goal, you need to develop a logical and focused plan to reach success. Commit your plan to writing and have every expectation of getting what you want. These in themselves are positive steps; you're dedicating energy to getting what you want. Persevere in your efforts . . . the best things in life do not just fall out of the sky.

ME—My prescription for success was to be hired as a human services administrator. My plan was simple: keep applying for jobs in the field, gain valuable experience, and keep moving up until a reasonably-sized organization saw the wisdom of hiring me as their executive director. However, I had not factored location and type of human service into my prescription. After an initial stint as an epidemiologist, I took a series of jobs with emotionally disturbed and delinquent inner city adolescents. Being a fair-haired, gentle suburban boy, I was like a fish out of water in the rough, urban environment. Bucks County, where I ultimately found a job at BARC, was a suburban community just like my hometown of Westfield, NJ. The match was perfect . . . because I'd honed my prescription for success.

YOU—

# MAKING ERRORS

Making errors and mistakes is the spice of life. In life, we are always called on to make decisions based on our experience and values. Decisiveness propels you forward, and forward is the only direction that time knows.

All the errors you make are learning opportunities; they help insure that you make better decisions in the future. Do not fret over poor decisions and do not let them freeze you into inaction. Learn from them . . . learn to be decisive. Then, whenever you make mistakes, your very decisiveness will propel you rapidly past them so you can go forward with renewed confidence and experience.

ME—Growing up in Westfield, NJ, my elementary school was one block from my home. One morning, feeling somewhat rambunctious, I decided to ride my bike to school. As I left my driveway, a very large commercial truck turned onto our street, and I proceeded to play "chicken" with it. Although the truck was moving too slowly to cause any harm, it blew its horn and I quickly swerved. This unfolded in full view of other students and the school crossing guard, who was obviously not amused. Later that same day, we had an assembly on safety during which the police sergeant publicly denounced my stunt, to my horrified embarrassment. That was one mistake from which I learned a great deal.

YOU—

# MAKING THE BEST FROM THE WORST

Many times, the best comes from the worst. When things are dismally troubled and hope seems to have taken a vacation, use the circumstance as an opportunity to succeed and move in a positive, meaningful direction. It only takes one person to be hopeful because that hope will become infectious, instilling hope in everyone.

There are always people who are quickly willing to throw in the towel and give up. These are people for whom a setback can prove insurmountable. Thankfully, there are always other people who never give up, who share their hope with all of us. They help us all find a way through the darkness. Whatever situation or circumstance you find yourself in, do not give up; find a way, move forward and live.

ME—Almost as soon as I began working at BARC, the agency suffered a major setback: a project they'd spent over a year developing was suddenly and without warning canceled. Needless to say, the agency's staff was very upset, even demoralized. I saw what I had to do . . . redirect everyone's energy into new endeavors. There was no point dwelling on what had happened; it was time to find a new project on which we could all move forward together. My plan worked. My hopefulness not only helped me in my transition to the agency, but helped others on the staff as well.

YOU—

# MASTERPIECE

Masterpiece is what you are . . . created in the image of G-d. You are a most beautiful entity who chooses to live, to help, and to move forward. Each of us controls where we are going even if we do not like where we are.

Don't move backward by dwelling on how you got to where you are and how miserable you are in such a location. Move forward by making choices that will improve your lot and make the world a better place. The road is often full of bumps and twists, but on occasion it may be smooth as glass. Accept the ups and downs and twists and turns; remember that forward movement is based on just such navigation. Accept each moment as it arrives, without judgment, and try to make the world a better place, for you and for everyone.

ME—I often think about the miracle of my body. How does my stomach, which digests all my food, know not to consume itself? How does my heart keep beating when it is not plugged into anything? How does my windpipe know to swallow only air and not food? How do my eyes work? Why did my soul select this body? Where is my soul going next? Why is our complex body so simple to understand once we know how it works? I don't have answers; I only have gratitude. Life has taken me on quite a journey and I keep navigating forward, more and more accepting of each glorious moment.

YOU—

# MOMENTS OFFER IT ALL

Moments are life's basic building blocks. How you meet and treat each moment defines who you are and how you live. Every moment abounds with strength and value; accept and relish it, and you will find all you ever want or need.

Allow the knowledge of this moment to move you toward your goal. Regardless of what you're doing right now, stop. Appreciate this moment. Acknowledge it with gratitude. Now, appreciate the next moment and the one right after it. Soon you'll discover that there's no turning back. Once you learn to live in the moment, you won't feel stuck ever again.

Each moment has more to offer than you can imagine. Your success is closely allied with how you use your moments. They are always waiting for you. It's up to you: use them and live, ignore them and exist.

ME—One day during the week Doug and I spent at the Buddhist Green Gulch Farm in Sausalito, CA, I experienced one of those very joyful, unforgettable moments. I'd come to lunch dressed in my yoga clothing. A twelve-year-old boy was there with his mother and our eyes met; I intuitively sensed that he was very amused with my white beard, white headpiece, and white outfit. We sat down at the same table, and I learned from the boy's mother that they were going through some rough times, recently arriving from out of state. David, the boy, was being home schooled, and he obviously looked forward to their once-a-week trip to the farm. We joked together and I let him show me how to use the giant coffee and tea makers in the dining room. Being with the boy, I was aware of how much he appreciated my interest in him . . . my desire just to be with him. "Why are you dressed all in white?" he asked me. I told him I like to shine and give my genuineness to others, just as I was doing with his mother and him. But inside, I knew that the shining light I radiated was being returned to me, ten-fold, by his smiles and laughter.

YOU—

# MUSCLES

Muscles become strong when we use them; people become strong the same way. After an exhausting workout, you feel sore and don't want to continue, but if you keep at it the next day, the pain eases, and then you feel so much stronger, and take pride in your strength and how you feel.

If you use your G-d given gifts and use your mind and body, you can achieve anything you desire; it is all there waiting for you. By repeating acts of human kindness and extending yourself into the world around you, you empower yourself to receive all that life has to offer. You become strong by being strong. You can always go a little further than you imagine and the rewards will always be waiting for you. You just need to begin.

ME—As a serious athlete in my youth, my muscles worked beautifully for my teammates and me. I was able to perform spectacular feats and received many accolades from my peers and coaches. Through daily training, my muscles were strong. Now, in the twilight of my career, I no longer perform any spectacular athletic feats; but I have learned over many years of training to perform daily human acts of kindness that are quite spectacular. One of the BARC residents, for example, was going through a very difficult sleepless period in his life, and would stay awake at night screaming uncontrollably. His housemates, their parents, the neighbors, his housemates' caseworkers, all wanted me to remove him from his home. I did not remove him, but I did get him different clinical interventions, including a new psychiatrist, and today, he is a happy, gainfully employed member of his community. Another resident, during manic psychotic breaks, broke every window in his group home on three occasions, costing the agency thousands of dollars. Today, he lives independently in the community, and is a quiet, calm, and caring individual.

YOU—

# NEED

Need can keep you from achieving what you want. You can become so focused on what you don't have and believe you need, that you forget that you already have what you really need. It is simply there for you to discover.

Abundance is everywhere; you only need to put yourself on the path that will enable you to see it and make it a part of every moment you exist. Look deep inside yourself to discover what it is you really need, and the path to it, will be illuminated, waiting for your gentle footsteps.

ME—Living a Spartan life free from possessions and the need for possessions has been very natural for me. It does help to be free of the obligations inherent in raising a family. It also helps to understand that I possess, thanks to the blessings of the Almighty, all that I really need.

YOU—

# NEGATIVE HABITS

Negative habits bring momentary, fleeting pleasures, but they cannot lead you to live a positive healthy life. Immersing yourself in negativity sacrifices all the wonder that is right at your fingertips. Getting immersed too deeply in negative habits (abusing drugs and/or alcohol, indulging in asocial behavior such as dismissing other people and acting disrespectfully) easily eradicates any memory that there is any other way, any other choice.

When you gain control of who you are and why you are here, you avoid destructive habits and build positive productive ones. Gaining control is not easy; it takes dedication and effort, but the rewards are great.

ME—One life-long negative habit is still with me... overeating. Intellectually, I know that the momentary pleasure I receive from eating too much does not enable me to lead a positive, healthy life; however, I haven't been able to overcome this hurdle. Over the course of my life, I've been on seven diets, losing a total of one hundred twenty-five pounds. I can remember how wonderful it felt to live a slimmer life, how much less of a burden it was to bear all that extra weight, yet I lack the self-control to maintain that healthier weight. The challenge has become even greater with age. As I write these words, I am determined to once again to keep off my extra weight. I know it takes dedication and energy, but I am ready. Let it be written, let it be done!

YOU—

# NO DAY IS A BAD DAY

Today, many things will happen, and the critical question is how you will use what happens. If you are in flow with whatever happens, then you will be able to use it to advance your goals without judgment or regret. Obstacles are occasions to energize and move forward, and not retreat and avoid.

You can move forward no matter what turns up on your path. Your positive attitude makes the details of what happens each day immaterial to your happiness.

ME—I have many days that do not go as well as I would like, or days when unpleasant things come up that I have to handle. For most of my life, I allowed the challenging days to diminish my appreciation of life. Today, I no longer minimize my appreciation of any day, no matter how challenging. No day is a bad day because I truly believe every day is a gift to enjoy. I do not come home and say "What a day! Boy, do I need a drink!" I come home and say, "Let's have a drink together . . . to toast the gift of life."

YOU

# YOU — NOW IS THE KEY

Now is the key to everything. Now is when you can begin to make things happen. Now is when you can turn your dreams into a real plan. Now is when you can resolve to do whatever you say you are going to do. Now is when you can use all of your experience and knowledge. Now is when you can make a difference and start saving the world. Now is when your vision starts to become clear. Now is the first moment of the rest of your life. Now is the time to act.

Yesterday is over and tomorrow is not here, so use now to become whatever you want to be.

ME—In the past, I made excuses . . . "I can't mow the lawn; I don't have time. I can't read this book; I'm too busy. I can't come to visit; I have appointments." Now I realize these were all excuses. Now I know I can make the time to accomplish anything I want; it is only a matter of prioritization, of asking what is important to me? Is it more important for me to watch television or go to the gym and exercise? Is it more important for me to eat a triple portion of spaghetti or lose the weight that keeps me fat? Is it more important that I go to work or stay home when I am sick? I know the answer to each question and simply need to make it a part of my conscious now.

YOU—

# OPPORTUNITY

Opportunity does not always come from positive experiences; many opportunities lie in things that annoy, frustrate and anger most people. If you examine your frustrating circumstances closely and with an open mind, you will discover an incredible opportunity awaiting you in each one. When you accept the task of turning something into a real and lasting value, you have accepted the opportunity to achieve through effort . . . because it is not a free ride. Anything worth accomplishing, takes effort. Without effort, there is diminished value, and when something has limited or no value, it is not worth achieving.

ME—I am most proud of an opportunity at BARC that annoyed, frustrated and angered people, but eventually turned into a lasting value for the organization and for me. The county administrator asked me to engineer a hostile takeover of a sheltered workshop run by a sister agency, which had engendered many vociferous complaints. I agreed—but only if I could take it over in a more orderly and open manner than the administration wished. Instead, the administrator approached another agency that performed the hostile takeover, angering many people. I was glad that I held to my position. Although I knew that BARC could easily help the troubled workshop, the way in which we were told to acquire the agency was inappropriate to me. In the end, my decision was respected by the county office and resulted in many years of positive considerations for BARC.

YOU—

# OPPORTUNITY THAT CHALLENGES

Opportunity that challenges you should always be welcomed because these moments help renew your confidence and, if successful, give you great pleasure.

But even if you fail, these opportunities are important. They reward you because you learn from the experience, and experience is what we need to succeed. Often, the most challenging times in life involve that which we care most about and value most: spouse, children, friends, work, and property. Their value doesn't derive from their cost or market value, but because of the heartfelt effort you invest in them. They challenge you to be your best, and when you rise to the challenge, you create emotional wealth, which in turn improves your life and everyone else's.

ME—One of my life's greatest challenges was raising my sons, Aaron and Justin. The effort in time, worry, money, and love was monumental; the pleasure I received from living with them and watching them grow was immeasurable. I had to dedicate a great deal of effort to keep them healthy; I stayed up sleepless nights with them when they were ill. I drove them from band practice to soccer games and back, bought them clothes they rapidly outgrew . . . yet it was all worthwhile. In fact, it led to the most rewarding and satisfying exhaustion I have ever known. All the expended energy has returned to me tenfold, just to see their happiness.

YOU—

# OTHER PEOPLE MIRROR YOU

Other people mirror you. If you examine deeply the traits of other people that annoy and frustrate you, you will find that in many respects, they are mirrors of who you are. Often, the people who annoy you most have the most to teach you, more than all the people that do not annoy you.

If you examine why you are annoyed with certain people, you will commonly find that it is not because of who they are, but how you react to who they are. The key is to get past your judgment of them and look for what they offer of value. Take the time to get past what you find annoying about them and focus on their humanity. Sometimes the value others offer is hidden, but with effort on your part, you can uncover it and make it a meaningful and important part of your life.

ME—When I first began working with people with developmental disabilities, I was able to acknowledge that they were unique human beings with the same traits that I possess: patience, impatience, fortitude, fear, overindulgence, kindness, trust, love of music, and love of people. The one trait I had difficulty with, however, was their simplicity. They were interested in the most basic things: When are we going to eat? When are going to go shopping? When are we going to have our dinner-dance? When are we getting paid? When are we going on vacation? I didn't dwell on these issues . . . or so I thought; I had more complex issues to sort out. But over time, I realized that the people I work with are right: the simplest questions are the most important questions, reflecting the issues that really count. It is never the "why," "what," or "where" that matters, but always the "when," . . . the incredible joy of anticipation and participation.

YOU—

# OUR ABILITIES

Our abilities far outweigh our disabilities. We are all blessed with certain abilities: sight, speech, hearing, touch, taste, smell, love, intuition, intelligence, feelings, and memory. Some of us have more abilities than others, but we all have certain gifts and it is with these gifts that we add value to the world.

There is no limit to what you can achieve once you plot your path, and take that first step. Limitations are not reasons to stop achieving; they are great opportunities to become whatever you want. If you do not have all of the aforementioned abilities, you can still be all that you want to be. Helen Keller never let her disabilities stand in the way of achieving whatever she wanted.

Once you stop using your disabilities as an excuse for not moving forward, you are ready to work with renewed gusto and purpose.

ME—One weekend, I participated in a statewide leadership course facilitated by a woman who was a quadriplegic. She required a full time aide to travel with her and take care of all her feeding, hygienic and transportation needs. Though she could only move her head and one hand, she did not describe herself as disabled. Instead, she recounted all the abilities she possessed: sight, speech, hearing, touch, taste, smell, love, intuition, intelligence, feelings and memory. "For me," she said, "my body works just fine." If attitude is everything, then her attitude allowed her to live a full and involved life. Her physical limitations did not prevent her from moving forward; if anything, her physical limitations made her message much more powerful.

YOU—

# PASSION

Passion is something you have, not something you find. Get in touch with your passion and you will be a brighter and happier person. You can find passion within the context of your own life. What are you passionate about: learning? sports? gardening? travel? driving?

Other people or events won't unleash it; you have to tap into it. Once you do, you'll find that you can imbue your every action with passion. Be passionate when you water your plants, when you clean your refrigerator, when you drive to the store. It will add a whole new dimension to your life.

ME—As a boy, I lived to play baseball. As a young adult, I was so passionate about jogging that I would sleep in my running clothes, in anticipation of my morning foray. I was very serious about succeeding in my career and pursued one job after another until I landed the one at BARC that offered me the opportunity to grow in many ways. I was passionate about caring and loving my sons. When they were small I could hardly wait to get home, to hug and hold them; a warm intense feeling flowed up my spine ending in an enormous ear-to-ear smile. Now I am passionate about enjoying and appreciating all the gifts I have always had: my body, my health, my environment, and others.

YOU—

# PATIENCE

Patience can make all the difference in your life, for when you are patient you cast away frustration and anger. Patience with yourself and others not only makes life easier for you but for everyone else as well.

When you meet people and events with anger and frustration, you become a victim of your anger and frustration. When you take people and events for who they are and how they flow, you become an accepted, integrated part of the universe. Use reason rather than reaction. Rely on thought rather than assumptions. Live proactively, not reactively.

Patience is a gift necessary for achievement. You will achieve your goals with patience, persistence, and effort. Anything of real value requires your effort, and encountering hurdles along the way is not a reason to stop or quit. If you expect immediate gratification, you will set yourself up for disappointment since anything lasting requires your patience. Anything you want can be yours if you are willing to work and wait.

ME—I grew up always in a hurry, for no particular reason. I ate fast, drove fast, talked fast, walked fast, and made love fast. I was a poor listener because I was in a hurry to either speak, or do something else. As my testosterone levels subsided and I matured, I came to understand the wisdom of patience and slowness. I learned that negotiation results in the best outcome when it is slow and deliberative. I learned that eating fast caused heartburn and flatulence (but I still stuff myself). I learned that fast driving was not particularly safe and caused me to receive traffic violations (but I still persist for the sheer pleasure I feel). I learned that talking fast often led to saying things I regretted. Today, no one would accuse me of talking too fast, if anything, I speak too slowly. I make love slowly and deliberately so that I can fully enjoy each moment of giving and receiving pleasure. Guided by ancient *tantric* wisdom, I know that it is always about the process, not the orgasmic climax. I have become, through much discipline and practice, a slower, better person.

YOU—

# PEOPLE COME AND GO

People come and go, but the good they spread is forever in memory. When you lose loved ones, the memory of their goodness is with you always; the light acts as a beacon to assist you in living, to fondly remember them with a glow.

Life is too short to worry and fear the loss of others. If you do, you are taking away from the abundant experience of living. Cherish all the people in your life; experience them fully, enjoy and take pleasure from their company, and cherish their memories after they are gone.

ME—All the people I have known that are now deceased have given me irreplaceable experiences, some good and others not so good. The one common thread running through all of their memories is that I learned invaluable lessons from the time I spent with them. The spirits of the ones I loved are with me always in a parallel universe (heaven to some); they communicate whenever a question or circumstance arises where their thoughtful and insightful counsel is needed. The spirits of my deceased friends, employees and acquaintances are not always with me, but the lessons they taught me about life are a part of who I have become. The gentle, patient spirit of my father is always most present when I am aggravated or impatient. The fun-loving spirit of my mother is most present whenever I start to take myself too seriously.

YOU—

# PEOPLE WHO HELP YOU

People who help you are the ones who challenge you, regardless of their motives. People who agree with everything you say or tell you what they think you want to hear will not help you to grow and achieve. You may prefer to spend time with people who are always kind to you, but they won't help you grow. The people who support your growth and achievement may make you uncomfortable, but they are giving you gifts you cannot at first appreciate.

When people hold you accountable for your actions, they assist you toward a freer, independent life; those who encourage and allow you to get away with things or accept your lame excuses assist you in remaining powerless and less empowered.

ME—As Executive Director of a large agency, I sometimes have to make life-and-death decisions for some of our residents, such as when to remove life support from a comatose patient. I need the people I work with to know they can talk to me honestly, without fear of reprisal. I welcome all opinions, even those I don't at first agree with because the more information I have, the more informed decisions I can make. We talk, plan, discuss, analyze, and finally we take action by consensus . . . though sometimes I have to make the final decision myself . . . a process that helps ensure that our conclusions are thoughtful. But this process wouldn't work if my employees didn't know how much I need them to speak from their hearts.

YOU—

# PERFECTIONISM

Perfectionism is a problematic human trait. If we were all perfect, we would all live in the Garden of Eden.

If you are a perfectionist, you relegate yourself to never being satisfied, and continual disappointment can lead you to unhappiness. If you want to experience joy, then you need to accept imperfection, especially in others. Life is full of ups and downs and if you wait for the perfect situation or perfect person to come along, you may have a very long wait indeed. Be grateful for all the imperfections life has to offer and get on with living. Imperfection challenges us to live.

ME—I have always been musically challenged and have had difficulty carrying a tune but it has not stopped me from enjoying listening to music, and from dancing. If nothing else, working with people with disabilities has taught me that perfectionism is temporary. I know that my current abilities could be snatched from me in an instant; or slowly, one by one, as I naturally age. I try to show other people the patience I hope they will accord me when I am old or disabled. From this perspective, we're all on a continuum of imperfection, and our position changes almost daily.

YOU—

# PERSEVERE

Persevere and live, give up and die. Living is all about movement and doing. As long as we live, our blood flows, and our body moves. Direct your motion toward creating achievement and good for you and the world. Perseverance is why humanity has progressed so far in every realm: technology, theatre, music, writing, invention, and spiritualism. Humanity has progressed because more people persevere in living than those who give up and die.

Whatever your goals, whatever your situation, keep moving, keep trying, keep progressing, keep living. You do not have to search for the gifts of life; they are always at your disposal, each moment. Take this moment to start appreciating these gifts by putting a smile on your face, and let the energy permeate to every pore and organ of your body.

ME—My greatest lesson with perseverance came from parents of children with disabilities. It is a lesson that stretches over more than a quarter of a century. Many of the BARC families who started receiving services when I first came to the agency in 1977 had sons and daughters the same age as Aaron and Justin (two and four years old). Like my sons, these children were in pre-school and day care programs. The only difference was that the BARC children took longer to learn how to walk, talk, play, think, and some never did. The BARC children, like mine, graduated into elementary and then high school. The BARC children, like mine, were in special education, although on different ends of the normal curve. The BARC children, like mine, stayed in school until the age of twenty-one, although the BARC children did not receive baccalaureate and masters degrees. The BARC children entered the work force in day programs, sheltered employment or part-time low paying community jobs. My children became an engineer and a teacher respectively, and quickly made a living wage. Most of the BARC children still live with their parents while my children live independently. The memory of physically carrying my children around, changing their diapers, and waking up at night to care for them, happened a very long time ago. For some BARC parents it is not a memory but still a daily occurrence. BARC parents are the ultimate in perseverance, the ultimate movers and doers. G-d bless them all!

YOU—

# PLANNING IS IMPORTANT BUT

Planning is important but moving forward gets things done. Connect with your desires and plan to accomplish them; then greet each day by proactively achieving what you want.

You may not reach your goal in one moment, one day, one week, one month, or one year. Just keep moving forward and you will get there. When you fill your moments with action, you fill your life with richness.

ME—As I write these words I plan to retire in seven years knowing full well that life has no guarantees. Events may dictate an earlier date or seven years hence I may feel like working another seven years. I considered a number of issues in planning when to retire: my current job satisfaction, retirement activities, my age, my finances, my needs, my eligibility status for retirement benefits and social security. As the seven-year countdown ensues I am proactively taking steps to insure that I do not become an inactive couch potato in retirement. These steps include the following: practicing and teaching yoga and meditation; writing books, reading, playing golf, investing my assets, and traveling. By discovering and doing now, what interests me I insure that my plan for the future is realistic and attainable.

YOU—

# POSITIVE PEOPLE

Positive people are powerful because they emit positive energy into the universe and invite others to join them. When you get excited about living, you radiate positive energy to others; you add significantly to all that is good and wonderful. Think positive and you will become one of the most powerful people.

Positive people distinguish themselves in how they talk, how they carry themselves, how they listen to other people, and by their general demeanor. Their positive energy can be manifested in a number of ways: by their presence, by their actions, by their intuition, by their helpfulness, by their sincerity, by their advice, by their silence.

ME—My best friend Doug has always been a positive person. After his parents were killed in a plane crash in 1962, he put his energy into becoming a better student, repeating his junior year of high school, and going on to become a Stanford graduate. After my wedding in 1971, he was diagnosed with cancer of the lymph nodes. He participated in a pilot study of a new treatment that prolonged life, married, had a daughter, divorced, remarried and had triplets. He started a construction business with a specialty in non-toxic termite extermination that is now prospering. Despite setbacks that may have stopped another person, Doug has always remained very positive about living, about enjoying the simple things, and loving nature. He emanates goodness for all the people who know him.

YOU—

# REALITY IS WHAT IS

Reality is simply what is; how we judge reality makes us who we are. If you view today as horrific, that is exactly how it will be for you. If you view today as splendid and full of opportunity and adventure, that is exactly how it will be for you.

Thinking does not change reality; it sets you on the path to making the most of reality for you and everyone around you. If you take the road to a positive, joyous outlook, you will never turn back to the dismal.

ME—When I graduated college, I had a sit-down with my father. I needed to ask him about life . . . what was it all about? He told me that the secret of life is never asking that question! His answer still conveys great wisdom. Whatever is . . . is. I know that neither I nor anyone else can change the way the world is and how people behave, but I can change how I think and behave. I often think of the analogy of the glass . . . is it half full or half empty? Though I have more years behind me than ahead of me, I always keep my glass of life's outlook half full, flowing with opportunity and possibility.

YOU—

# REGARDLESS HOW HIGH THE GOAL

Regardless how high the mountain, it can always be climbed. The closer you get to the top of the mountain, the more attainable it becomes. The first men to reach the summit of Mount Everest sacrificed a great deal, and, as they approached the summit, the effort became more and more difficult. Their persistence was rewarded with success.

Similarly, no matter how high your goal is, it can be achieved through your persistence in the face of many difficult challenges. Like the Mount Everest climbers, you may experience great weariness in pursuing what you want; this is the best part of the reward because it indicates that you have already had a great deal of success in pursuing what you want. Most importantly, it indicates that you have been living life, not just existing.

ME—One of the highest mountains I ever had to climb, professionally, was overseeing the building of a new production center in Warminster, PA to support over two hundred workers with handicaps. We had to plan everything from scratch . . . conduct a feasibility study about running a capital campaign to raise money for the project, locate land to purchase, hire a contractor, get the necessary state and federal approvals. Each individual step was an enormous undertaking . . . for me and for the agency. Coordinating all the various activities seemed, at times, to require an almost superhuman effort. In the end, we raised over $1.7 million, but encountered problems at every stage. We even had to file a lawsuit against a contractor. But eventually, we reached the mountaintop . . . we moved in. My reward was knowing that people with developmental disabilities would have a place to work long after I was gone.

YOU—

# REPEATING GOOD

Repeating good will snowball into more good. Whenever we are kind, it creates value. Whenever you repeat a kindness, you create more value, and whenever you make a habit of kindness, you change the world.

There is never a limit on how much good will you can create. Every moment contains the potential. When you're driving, let someone cut in front of you. When you are waiting in a long line to buy something, start a conversation with the person behind you, and let him or her in front of you if they have fewer items. Make a habit of always giving loose pocket change to street performers or beggars. The more good you sow, the more you will reap in your own joy and happiness.

ME—As an agency director, I have to keep a close eye on the budget; we always struggle to have enough funds. For years I resisted adding new holidays to those our agency already observed since we have to pay double time for residential coverage during holidays. But as our population of African-Americans increased, I realized that it was disrespectful not to recognize Martin Luther King Junior's birthday. In the end, I bit the fiscal bullet and the Board agreed to honor Dr. King. When I announced this decision to our staff at one of our facilities, they burst into applause and cheers. Though I'd never imagined I'd be rewarded in this way, it remains a moment I will never forget.

YOU—

# RESPONSIBILITY

Responsibility is the key to being free. When we accept responsibility for who we are and how we interact with the world, then whatever we become will be more true to who we really are and how the world perceives us.

To be free is to be true to your core self . . . who you are, who you were meant to be. But freedom takes effort and does not come without sacrifice. Effort is needed to really analyze critically who you really are; it usually requires some skilled counseling or therapy. The sacrifice comes from the discomfort and anguish the critical analysis will inevitably cause.

ME—For years, I paid no attention to the sexual orientation of my staff. It never came up, and I never raised the issue. Then, a mutual acquaintance asked my partner Jean to accompany him to a Chamber of Commerce dinner-dance. It turned out that he was gay, and he knew that his partner would not be welcome at the evening event. I was very touched by this. I began to realize how the issue of gay rights had been ignored at my agency. On my own, I proposed an all-inclusive health coverage plan for same sex and opposite sex single partners that received Board approval. Now, the gay staff members at my agency feel free to talk about their partners. They are taking responsibility for who they are, as I took responsibility to make our agency a truly welcoming workplace.

YOU—

# SUCCESS IS NOT MONEY, FAME, AND POWER

Success is not having money, fame, power, or the praise of others. Success comes to those who use their G-d given gifts to make themselves and the world a better place. When you add value to your life and the lives of others, it is far more valuable than all the gold in Fort Knox.

Success is knowing who you are, and acting on your natural ability to use every moment's opportunities to spread your light to the world in appreciation for the light you take from the abundance all around you. When your path in life is devoted to finding purpose and value, then you will find unimaginable success and joy.

ME—I have always been amazed at the value people put in seeing, being with, and knowing famous people such as movie stars, musicians, and athletes. The hand-full of famous people I have met are not very glamorous and not very happy; their lives, as we read in the newspapers, are often filled with alcohol, drugs and/or infidelities. Real success does not come from money, fame, and power; it comes from being connected to your inner core, who you really are. I do not look for my heroes on television, in movies or in glamour magazines; my heroes are closer to home: my parents, my sons, my dear relatives, my partner, my close friends, parents at BARC, and most importantly... me!

YOU—

# SUCCESS NEEDS FAILURE

Success does not come without failure. Failure creates life's greatest opportunities for success. Failure simply shows you the path not to travel; it obliges you to eliminate one road in your quest for what you want.

Remember that when night is its darkest, dawn is already coming. Defeat is only a way of thinking and feeling; it never has to be a way of being. Success is always waiting. Are you ready to start succeeding?

ME—As part of my sons' education in Piscataway, NJ, they had an elective to compete in Odyssey of the Mind (OM). They made some halfhearted attempts in grade school and during their early high school all of which were competitive failures. In 1992, when Aaron was a senior and Justin was a sophomore, they decided to get serious. They assembled a team of fellow students to plan, build and run five model cars, each powered by a different source of propulsion. Drawing on their past failures, they knew what was expected and anticipated obstacles. As a result, they entered the competition with renewed gusto. Their reward: they finished first in the county, first in the region, first in the state, and eighth in the world.

YOU—

# TAKE A HIGHER PERSPECTIVE

Take a higher perspective when things are getting you down. By looking up instead of down, you elevate yourself and everyone you come in contact with. If you do not know where you are going or what you want, then any change will get you down because it is all you have to focus on. By looking and accepting the bigger picture, you keep life in focus and find that change can be very gratifying. Taking the higher perspective can lead you away from your fears and make life so much more full. By looking at life from a higher perspective that is different from your narrow subjective perspective, you elevate your appreciation and gratitude for what you have and just how grand it is.

ME—During the 1980's and 1990's, the human services industry experienced some very dramatic changes in the delivery of service. It moved from a client—dependent model to a self-determined model, and many BARC staff members had a difficult time adjusting to this paradigm shift. One of my department directors summed it up beautifully for her staff: you each have to decide if you are on the train, at the station, or on the tracks. If you are on the train, you will thoroughly enjoy the ride. If you are still at the station, you have some decisions to make. If you are on the tracks, you will be run over by the train. Those on the train stayed employed with the agency. Some station dwellers got on the train and some left the agency. Everyone on the tracks was terminated from employment or left the agency.

YOU—

# TAKE DOWN YOUR PSYCHIC WALL

Take down your psychic wall and let life in. Living is all about being moved and feeling. Yes, it will sometimes hurt, but so many other times it will be wonderful. Let in all that life has to offer . . . the noise, sadness, happiness, thrills, disappointments, and joy. Life should not be viewed from behind a fortified wall or from the bleachers; it is meant to be lived and experienced. Take down your psychic wall, come out of the bleachers and be alive, right now, this moment.

To be human is to have defense mechanisms, but to overuse them can take a great deal out of living. Everything needs to be moderated. A hermit does not experience the pain caused by human interaction, but he also never feels the extraordinary pleasure of friendship, love, and social activities.

ME—My psychic walls were and still are made of withdrawal and disconnection. When I feel stressed, I retreat to my own self-imposed isolation. I have learned not to overuse my psychic walls. Instead, I use them in moderation, cherishing and enjoying my times of disconnection from people when I go deep within myself and connect with nature, and all that is around me. After twenty-four hours of retreat, however, I need to be with other people . . . to interact, to socialize, to work. The secret, I now know, is to be able to live with yourself and with others. If I was not comfortable with myself, I know I would not be comfortable in the company of others.

YOU—

# TAKE LIFE IN THE PRESENT

Take life as it comes because you really have no other choice. You cannot predict the future and cannot recreate or live in the past, so why not make of the best of the present?

How many times have you worried about something that turned out to be rather pleasant? How many times have you avoided something that you ended up embracing? How many times have you said "no" to something only to regret it?

Life is a series of ups and downs. It is up to each of us to accept and take life as it comes, even its darkest valleys. What is heaven to one person can be hell to another; it is always a question of how you view it, and how you take it.

ME—Every few months I attend the quarterly meeting of the Pennsylvania Association of Resources for People with Mental Retardation, a professional association of agencies providing services for people with Developmental Disabilities throughout the state. A few days before each meeting I begin to ruminate on how many things I have to do at work, how I cannot afford to take a whole day off to discuss issues I already know about, and how long the drive to Harrisburg will take. Invariably I overcome my ruminations and attend the meeting. Each time I am very pleased that I have attended to hear and gain insight into all the subtleties of the issues unobtainable through other sources, and more importantly to socialize and enjoy the camaraderie of my peers and colleagues. On the occasions when I do not attend, I miss the many gifts of being there.

YOU—

# TAKING CARE OF YOURSELF

Taking care of you is not being selfish. Being selfish involves not giving anything to others, and not making an effort for others. Taking care of you means living a healthy life that includes eating a good diet, exercising and having plenty of mental stimulation. Clearly, you can take care of yourself while still becoming involved with others. The two are not mutually exclusive.

Taking care of yourself allows you to be available for others, to spread your happiness to others, to shine your light on the world. Being selfish prevents your light from shining. If you take care of yourself, you'll heal the world at the same time that you heal yourself.

ME—The American Heritage Dictionary defines selfish as "concerned chiefly or only with oneself." I think we are all selfish in various degrees, and a certain degree of selfishness is necessary. If we're not concerned at all with ourselves how could we possibly live, be available to others and spread happiness? I believe that I make a larger positive contribution to the world by being happy with myself than by simply doing tasks for others. My selfishness is all about giving myself pleasure, and a great deal of that pleasure comes from seeing other people smiling and happy. My effectiveness as an administrator and father doesn't derive from all the work or tasks I perform but rather from the happiness I give to others by being with them, and showing them that I care.

YOU—

# TASK COMPLETION

Task completion . . . getting things done . . . is a blessing. There is always so much to do. If life is to move forward, it requires a commitment on your part to finish what you begin. The first step is to decide what needs to get done, what is attainable. Next, determine in what order you will tackle the tasks. Set realistic goals for yourself so that you are sufficiently challenged without letting yourself become overwhelmed.

Learn to appreciate completing each individual task along the way to achieving your larger goal. You can even reward yourself. Feeling good about what you've accomplished will help counterbalance the effort that goes into completing tasks . . . effort that is always well worth it.

ME—I consider myself blessed with the desire to always finish what I start. As a young man I never left a model airplane half-built; I never mowed half the lawn. As an adult, I bring my penchant for task completion to the world of work in a number of areas: I always leave my desk cleared when I go home; I work whatever time it takes to get assignments and tasks done long before they are due; I set timelines and create expectations for my staff when it comes to completing tasks. I take great pleasure in making lists and crossing things off the list when they are accomplished. Task completion is one of my many blessings.

YOU—

# THE BEST TIME TO BE POSITIVE

The best time to be positive is when there is no reason to be so. By always being positive, even in the midst of the most difficult challenges or profound sadness, the world becomes more positive. Being positive does not mean the negativity in the world is vanquished; it simply insures that you and all that you touch is nudged toward success, gratitude and joy.

Think of yourself as a lamp for all who wallow in darkness. Be a beam of hope for all who allow despair to dominate their lives, and most importantly of all, be a role model for the one person who is most important . . . you!

ME—How many people stop to say a word to a toll taker? That's exactly what I did, for twenty years, when I traveled on Route 202 from New Jersey to Pennsylvania. I had read an article on the lonely, stressful life of toll takers, who meet thousands of people for seconds at a time. Because I saw the same toll taker every morning, he and I struck up brief conversations . . . about the weather, the road, and the traffic. He started to greet me as "Cap" which at first I thought was short for "captain," but came to realize it was in response to the caps I always wore. This exchange of a few words brightened both our days. I still greet those who take my tolls. Even if they don't respond, which happens most of the time, I feel better.

YOU—

# THE BIG PICTURE

The big picture, when you can keep it in mind, allows you to rise above all the small annoyances that bring you down: your neighbor's loud music early on Saturday morning, disrespectful and ungrateful children, your boss who asks you to do too much, your spouse who watches too much television.

Being aware of the big picture allows us to keep things in perspective. When we think of the miracle of life on its grandest scale, we embrace the gift of life, our connection to each other, the earth, the universe, and all living things. Appreciating the miracle of our place in the big picture, all the little annoyances of daily living become just that . . . little annoyances, part of the little picture. By training ourselves to look beyond the little picture in which we live our daily lives, we can enhance our lives and those around us.

ME—I recently was guided to a science web site, "Powers of Ten" that dramatically showed what the big picture means. It displays a series of pictures. First, it shows how small a spot of light our galaxy, the Milky Way, occupies in the universe. Next we see how small a spot of light our solar system and sun occupy in the Milky Way. Next we see our planet, earth, as a dot in the solar system; then, the earth as viewed from the moon. This is followed by a sequence of enhanced satellite photos: of North America, the Northern United States, Pennsylvania, a county in Pennsylvania, a town in Pennsylvania, a tree in that town, one branch of that tree, one leaf, the cells in that leaf, and finally subatomic particles in that cell. Viewing this sequence, I understood how tiny we really are in the huge scheme of things. I also realized that everything I was worrying about was much tinier than I was, and let it go.

YOU—

# THERE'S A REASON

There's a reason behind everything you do. There's a reason that explains the order in which you do things. There's a reason you don't do certain things. There's a reason you have certain dreams and fantasies.

When you explore and understand your reasons for what you do, you are on the road to really doing what you want. Choose to act on those things for which you have the most compelling reason to act . . . reasons that matter and will enhance your life and the lives of those around you. Activities that fulfill you and nourish your soul are the activities you want to continue. That which causes you pain can be diminished or eliminated. By knowing the reasons behind what you do and do not do, you get closer to making choices that will change your life for the better.

ME—As I write this book I have almost thirty years of experience as Executive Director of BARC and I am enjoying seeing the fruits of my labor: a highly regarded, adequately funded agency; a high level and high regard for continual quality improvement; sophisticated support services in finance, human resources, and quality resources. There are many reasons why my marriage with BARC has been so fulfilling: the culture of a kind suburban environment similar to the environment where I grew up; being in charge of a growing and viable organization; working with and for people who really care about others; never questioning, at the end of each day, the product (i.e., people with disabilities) I am supporting; the complexity and challenge of providing so many services to so many people. I enjoy training younger managers to take over the reins after I retire, and I hope I am infusing them with the same good reasons for making BARC the organization to fulfill their career dreams, just like it did for me.

YOU—

# THE WORLD DOES NOT OWE YOU

The world does not owe you anything. You are a unique creature connected to a vast universe. The world is not for or against you or anybody else . . . it just is what it is.

Making excuses for not getting what you want will not get you what you want. Anything you want and is worth getting requires your focused effort. Success comes to those who dream, plan to fulfill those dreams, and take the action required. Each moment is a chance to exercise those actions, to move forward, to get the results that you desire. Your success comes from your thoughts and attitude, not anybody else's. You determine the path you take. Take the path of success and fulfillment; be prepared and motivated to take on any challenge, cross any chasm, jump any hurdle, and tackle any obstacle.

ME—I have never felt the world or anybody owed me anything. When people ask me why I married Shirley, the only answers I can offer are that my mother really liked her, most of my friends were getting married, and Shirley wanted to get married. It's also true that Shirley and I did love each other even though we had very different personalities. The twenty-five year marriage had many happy years, many not so happy years, and produced two wonderful sons. I have learned, thanks to Jean, to view the marriage more positively. It is much more rewarding to reflect on the positive rather than the negative, or at least to have a balanced reflection on both the good and the bad. Who I married, and what I did in my life, was all decided by me. I have made many decisions, some good, some not so good, but they all were mine. I make no excuses for any decision I have ever made.

YOU—

# THE WORLD IS FULL

The world is full . . . it is up to you to live in its abundance. By wallowing in grief and worry, you deprive yourself of what already is available to you: beauty, fulfillment, awe, connection, joy, and quiet. Your current circumstance is the perfect launching platform to begin to fully appreciate it all. Take the step and become part of the game, not an observing bystander. It is all there for you, all the time, every moment of every day. It is all waiting for you . . . it never goes away . . . you just need to recognize it. You can move as high as you would like . . . you only need to take the first step. The first step is very simple; begin by observing and becoming lost in the incredible beauty of the sunrise and sunset, or squirrels at play, or the gracefulness of birds in the sky.

ME—When I watch the news on television, I get the impression that the world is a dismal, hateful planet wracked with violence. When we are not busy killing and maiming each other, nature supplies the storms and avalanches to spread misery. I've come to realize that television sensationalizes the news in the negative. It tends to report action and violence for the purpose of garnering market share. In reality, the world is a very peaceful, comfortable, miraculous place. If we were to place a camera in most places of the world for twenty-four hours, we would not see violence and mayhem. Because of this, I no longer watch the news on television although I still read about world events. My world is very far away from world events because it consists of living each day without competition, rancor, and violence. If my presence helps one person, then I have helped the whole world.

YOU—

# THERE IS ALWAYS HOPE

Hope is an essential ingredient in our lives. Without hope, it would be difficult to get through the day. Like water, we need hope to nourish us through lean times. With something to look forward to, many of us can persevere even in the face of hardship.

But hope can't survive on it's own. Hopefulness needs to be accompanied by action. Otherwise, hope remains a thought in your mind. Translating hope into reality means putting forth effort. Only you can make things happen; only you can realize your hopes. Let hopeful thoughts sustain you as you dig in and set out to make real all that you hope for.

ME—My career hope was very clear. I wanted to be an executive director of a good-sized nonprofit agency where I could grow the service and apply my administrative and supervisory skills. For years, as I nurtured this hope I also updated my resume, read want ads, mailed countless letters, went on innumerable interviews, and took six jobs before the offer came through from BARC. Hope propelled me to take action; taking action fed my hopes eventually leading to my dream job.

YOU—

# THINKING AND ACTING

Thinking and acting are intimately tied to each other. Acting without thinking can be chaotic and purposeless. Thinking without acting can lead to rumination, worry, anxiety, and self-defeating behavior. We all know, for example, that impulsive actions, undertaken without forethought, can cause much grief. People who act on their thoughts and feelings without considering the consequences can cause grave harm, like the mother who hits her children out of frustration, never stopping to think about the long-term consequences of her behavior. By the same token, people who think about doing something but never do create heartache for themselves and others. A man who thinks about helping his wife take care of their kids but never makes good on his word most likely embitters his wife, and finds himself filled with self-recrimination. Both action and thought are necessary, and neither is sufficient alone.

ME—My speeding tickets and car accidents all came from actions absent logical thinking. I knew and still know that the more times you exceed the speed limit, the higher your chances are of receiving a speeding ticket. I knew and still know that in wet conditions, slower speed and more caution is in order. I knew and still know that whenever you take your eyes off the road, you increase your chances of having an accident. All my acts of stupidity occurred due to the absent of forethought: I once pretended, for the amusement of my friends, to bear down on some pigeons in the road, never thinking that they all would not be able to get out of the way. When driving home from school, I once took a long look at a woman walking along the road, and was unable to stop in time to avoid hitting the car in front of me that had stopped to make a left hand turn. Hitting and killing pigeons was an event in my history that troubles me to this day; if I had thought before impulsively acting, the result would have been much more acceptable. Likewise, impulsively looking without forethought at a woman or anything else unrelated to driving or safety is never a very good idea.

YOU—

# THIS IS YOUR BIG MOMENT

This is your big moment since every moment is your big moment. Take this moment to change your life into something meaningful, joyful, and full of awe and gratitude. This day is the moment you have always wanted, dreamed of, envisioned, and wished for. It is here now and it is very real. It is not perfect but it is all you need. Take it, cherish it, utilize it, be grateful for it, and most of all enjoy it. Make it great, gorgeous, huge, glorious, spontaneous, heartfelt, powerful, awe—inspiring, unbelievable, ineluctable, beyond words, heavenly . . . a gift. The first step in making today your big moment is believing, with your head and your heart, that you and everything around you is truly miraculous.

ME—It took me over fifty years to truly realize and live the concept that every moment is my big moment. My first step was to recall all my past fond memories: playing and winning at soccer and baseball; socializing with friends and traveling all over the world; falling in love; my Bar Mitzvah; my wedding; my early years of marriage; the birth of my sons; numerous employment related occasions. By taking pleasure in my memories, I was able to begin to see the wisdom of moment-by-moment living. What I remembered best was the memory of coming home from work each day to see my infant sons, Aaron and Justin. When I left work and got into my car, my body would light up with warm love and joy at the expectation of seeing and holding my two precious boys. The joy of having them, being with them, and loving them made every day a wonderful experience. As I recalled these memories, I began to recreate the feelings they engendered in the present . . . with what was happening each moment: sensing all the gifts of nature; working with diverse personalities; listening to music; socializing with friends; eating; taking a shower.

YOU—

# THIS MOMENT YOU CAN DECIDE

This moment is the moment you can decide to move forward. Allow this moment to be the last moment of your difficulties, the last moment of your frustration and despair. Allow this moment to be the beginning of your new happiness.

Begin this moment to fulfill all your dreams, to do all that you ever wanted to do. Begin this moment as the best you can be. Let all your past disappointments be part of history, for that is all they truly are. Action unfolds in the present. Don't miss out on it. Be there. You are the only one who can make change for yourself . . . and you can start . . . this very moment.

ME— A staff manager at BARC had been under-performing for months and I was obliged to send him a warning letter. Based on my experience with other under-performing staff members, I was quite certain this person would quit rather than wait to be fired. To my pleasant surprise, he seized the moment, and turned his performance completely around. He put his disappointing performance behind him and became a consistent steady performer who remained a valued employee at BARC until his retirement.

YOU—

# THOUGHTS ARE POWERFUL

Thoughts are very powerful, and it is up to you to insure that they remain positive. Frustration, worry, anxiety are all thoughts. Thoughts such as, "I can't do it," or "I'm anxious about that," can imprison and turn all the beauty of life into gloom. Positive thoughts, such as, "I can," and "I will," can enlighten and turn an otherwise gloomy circumstance into beauty and wonderment.

Your thoughts control who you are; you control your thoughts. Tune in to what you're thinking. What kinds of statements do you make about yourself? About others around you? About the circumstances you're facing? By paying attention to what you are thinking and controlling those thoughts, you can change things dynamically for the better. Would you spend money on a car you did not like, or sit for hours in an uncomfortable chair? Probably not! So why would you think unsavory, negative thoughts? Instead, fill your mind with positive, creative thoughts that make you a better person and give value to others. Regardless of your situation, use your mind to solve problems, find new ways, and take new paths. Let go of old, worn-out ideas. Think about beauty, peace, serenity, and love.

ME—In meditation I have learned to focus on my breath. Life is all about breathing in and breathing out . . . taking the world in and giving out to the world. Over time I have been able to generalize the calm, tranquil feeling I derive from meditation to everyday experiences. No matter how difficult the challenge, things always work out in the end. Many years ago, long before I started to meditate, I would take a day off from work to spend with my cousin Sylvia in New York City. Our greatest pleasure came from leisurely walking through the busy, weekday streets of Manhattan. My mind was clear of all anxiety, stress, and worry, and full of joy and fun. I often recount this memory in the present to clear my mind of all negative and harmful thoughts.

YOU—

# TRANQUILITY

Tranquility is a state of relaxation, a state free of anxiety, worry, depression, and tension. Being tranquil brings you and every one you meet joy and pleasure. Bring peace to the world through your peace, through your relaxed mien, through your gentle and kind thoughts.

When you are relaxed, you bring positive energy to yourself, and allow yourself to be whatever you want to be. Physiologically, it's a gift to your body as well. A tranquil mind can lower your blood pressure, and help prevent many organ diseases. Tranquility can be achieved through many avenues in addition to yoga and meditation. It is all a matter of what you love and enjoy: gardening, writing, reading, music, sports, golf, or perhaps gourmet cooking.

ME—For me, meditation is the greatest path to tranquility. With practice, I have been able to expand the peacefulness I achieve when I meditate so that it infuses my spirit every day. When I'm tranquil, I feel my connection to nature and the universe. It has allowed me to be more present with other people and become a better listener. People have commented on my calmness and I sense that they respect and honor it. It certainly has assisted me to discover who I am and what I want.

YOU—

# TURN IT AROUND

Turn it around. It's one of the secrets of life. No matter how bad a day or a moment may start, it is within your power to make it different, to turn it around.

Events are not intrinsically good or bad; they are just events, or the way that things are. What is . . . is. We perceive events as good or bad. And you are free to perceive them any way you like. That's how you can turn things around. Find a new way to think about something that happened, or about another person. If you want positive outcomes, it is up to you to make it happen by thinking positively as you go through the events of your life. Just because something begins one way doesn't mean it's fated to end that way. You have the power to turn it around.

ME—Experience has been my best enabler in turning things around. BARC and I have been sued many times during my tenure. The first time I was served legal papers from the County Sheriff, I was totally shocked and allowed it to ruin the day, the week, the month, and the year. I was concerned about having adequate insurance coverage, negative publicity, the reaction of the Board of Directors, and my own security. Going through the first lawsuit, I learned that, like so much in life, it was simply an event that had a standardized drill that must be learned. By the third lawsuit, I knew the drill quite well, and was able to turn it around. By thinking about lawsuits as events that occur in administration, I was able to take positive steps to prevent them and more successfully fight them as they occurred.

YOU—

# USE TIME TO ACCOMPLISH

Use time wisely to do what you want to accomplish. Use progressive activity to achieve what you desire, never letting go of your gratitude for each and every moment. By doing things now and not putting them off, you will feel more fulfilled and energized.

If you cannot accomplish all that you would like to in a given time period, don't let it get you down. Take pleasure and pride in what you did do, and be satisfied that the rest can be achieved another time. Time needs you to fill it up; you do not need time to fill you up. Time is your friend, not your enemy . . . if you learn to use it well.

ME—Using time wisely means being organized and being a good manager. Using time wisely means anticipating obstacles that may throw off your schedule. Using time wisely means having a realistic sense of how much can be done in a certain time period, and not expecting too much or too little. Whenever I have a new task, I try to complete it as soon as possible, thus keeping the piles of undone tasks off my desk. I rarely do something the last minute, just before it is due. I always anticipate that the computer may go down, the copier will not work, or the mail will get lost. I always set deadlines for my staff whenever I request something so they can also plan their time accordingly.

YOU—

# WE ALL CAN GET IN THE GAME

We all can find a reason to achieve or we can back off from all that comes our way; the choice is ours. When the game is on the line, some of us huddle on the bench while others ask for the ball. What course do you follow? What course is right for you?

Every time you are sad or discouraged, recognize it as a time to overcome your impulse to withdraw and do the opposite . . . get involved. Rather than throw in the towel, find a way to accomplish what you want. We each must find a reason to succeed, a reason to be involved. Otherwise, life is so uninteresting, filled with nothing more exciting than "what could have been!" Make life what it is meant to be . . . full of glorious meaning, accomplishment, and progress.

ME—During my career at BARC, a new staff member, Tom, compiled a seventy-page invective, accusing the residential staff of gross misconduct, which he then presented to the Board of Directors and me. Tony, the Residential Director, was extremely upset and offered me his resignation, which I immediately refused. The ball game was on the line and I stepped up to the plate in support of Tony. Opening an investigation, we soon discovered that Tom had pulled the same stunt in his three previous jobs. Once this was uncovered, Tom left the agency . . . and in fact, never worked in our industry again. Years later, the ball game was once again on the line, but this time it was my neck in the noose. A hateful board member was hell bent on removing me from my employment after twenty years on the job. He approached Tony to take over my job; Tony refused and the palace coup attempt failed.

YOU—

# WE ALL HAVE GIFTS

We all have strengths and weaknesses. Some of us are great musicians, some of us are great intellects, and some of us are great athletes. Maybe we have a great smile or laugh; maybe we know how to genuinely empathize. We all are born with certain gifts.

Whatever our gifts, whether they be many or few, it is up to us to use them for our own happiness and the happiness we can give to the world and others. The nasty alternative is to wallow in all that we do not have and allow jealousy, pride, worry, and fear to dominate how we live.

Make an inventory of all your strengths and the gifts you do have. Appreciate them, strive for improvement, and never forget all you have.

ME—I believe that most communication is nonverbal. I have come to more fully appreciate the incredible gift so many of us have in regard to nonverbal communication. I marvel at the gift of knowing what someone is thinking by slight variations in their eyebrows, eyes, lips, mouth, skin color, arms, hands, fingers, legs, head, forehead, cheeks, ears, torso, pelvis, and odor.

YOU—

# WE LIVE WITH CHANGE

We live in a world of constant change, but this does not mean that our world is unstable. We simply need to be adaptable in order to succeed. You need to go with the flow, adapt to the situation, and allow for decisions that counter the conventional wisdom.

Adapting does not require compromising your values and goals; it means strengthening your values and goals by making a confident decision, one that you know in your heart is the right one. Rather than focus on blaming and complaining, concentrate on changing your course so you can reach a satisfactory solution. Each time you successfully adapt, you will strengthen your positive energy and resolve.

ME—In the late 1980's, the paradigm in mental health and mental retardation services changed dramatically: instead of agencies deciding how to take care of the people they served, individuals would now be deciding how they would like to be taken care of and by whom. I had no difficulty with empowering our clients, especially since some of them had been treated for so long as second-class citizens. But I did have a problem when some of our group home residents began requesting to live more independently without twenty-four hour supervision. I could not envision how folks who had to be reminded over and over again to put on a coat, or turn off the stove, could live independently. But the problem was mine, not theirs: I needed to adapt, to go with the flow, even though it went against what I had always believed. I did and I have absolutely no regrets. All the people now living independently have thirty hours of supervision each week from a staff member, and are living stable, quality lives.

YOU—

# WE TAKE OTHERS BY LISTENING AND FEELING

We take the world in by inhaling and give ourselves back to the world by exhaling. Likewise, we accept others by listening and feeling, and allow others to accept us by talking and feeling. Life is not a one-way street. Life is all about giving and receiving.

Accept others by listening to them, feeling with them and giving them solace. Accept yourself by opening up your heart to others and allowing them to listen and feel with you.

Do you share your innermost thoughts with others or do you keep yourself locked up inside? Do you allow others to share their most innermost thoughts with you, or do you change the subject to sports or the weather whenever the conversation turns personal? Living life to the fullest is not just about inane banter; it is about engaging with others. Life is a two-way street. Allow all your inner treasures to be shared with others, and allow them to share all their inner treasures with you.

ME—I first started to become a better listener shortly after beginning to work at BARC. A woman, who was my age, came to talk to me about whether her son, who was the same age as my son Justin, was a candidate for our early intervention program. She described him as significantly delayed in terms of his physical and mental development, and told me how much care he required. I could feel myself listening with a new quality of engagement. She'd penetrated my shield; her story had touched me. As my eyes welled up, I realized that I was finally learning how to really listen

YOU—

# WHAT YOU GIVE IS WHAT YOU GET

What you give is what you get. What you give to the world is what the world will give back to you. If you sow complaints and negativity, the world will give them back to you in kind. If you sow happiness and joy, the world will give you back happiness and joy.

Look in the mirror; who you are? How other people see and experience you determines how they will treat you. If you are forlorn and despondent, people will avoid you or give you more sorrow. If you are always smiling, people will come to you and give you more smiles and light. All positive energy in the world and all the best things in life begin with you . . . your attitude, your persona. Everything you always wanted is always available. You simply need to make the effort to get it.

ME—I have always been attracted to upbeat people... people who are exciting to be with, people who make things happen, people who smile rather than frown. When I am smiling, more strangers will say hello. When I am smiling, the whole world seems to smile back. When I am smiling, I am free to do whatever I choose, and what I choose will always be a joy to others and me. I stay away from chronic complainers; they are dealing with twisted *kharma* and seem to bring negativity to themselves simply by anticipating it.

YOU—

# WHEN YOU ARE STUCK

When you are stuck, take the time to remember a time when you were effective. How did you get "unstuck"? How can you break out of a stalemate and begin to take effective action?

Sometimes the issue is not easily unstuck and requires enormous effort or even medical intervention. At the very least, most issues require your undivided attention and time.

When you start with a plan that worked in the past, you can be reasonably sure it will work again. That's how you take the first step toward creating new momentum for the task at hand. Momentum is infectious and, in time, will carry over into all areas of your life. Your confidence and certainty will grow with each new achievement, and the hurdles you overcome will empower you even more. Rome was not conquered in one day and your success does not happen overnight. It takes effort and you need to take the first step. Success does not come in leaps and bounds; it begins with that first small step.

ME—I was stuck in the mental illness of depression. The only tasks I could rouse myself to perform, however minimally, were those obligations I had to family and work. Although I dreaded even the most minimal tasks, once performed, they were never as horrible as my mind conjured. Once I realized my denial of being mentally ill and accepted it for what it was, I was able to take the first step on my road to recovery. Over time and with enormous effort I was able to receive the help I needed and the symptoms began to decrease and eventually disappear. Whenever I am stuck I remember the steps I took with depression accompanied by patience, time, and my undivided attention. The memory of my success always provides me with the knowledge of what I must do to break out of any stalemate.

YOU—

# WHAT'S HOLDING YOU BACK?

What's holding you back from reaching your goals may be any of a number of problems. Denial is a powerful human defense mechanism that keeps people from realizing their dreams. When we deny something, we pretend it isn't there. The first step in dealing with denial is to accept its existence in your life. The next step is to recognize it as a weakness that is holding you back from achieving all that you want to be.

Other factors may be hindering your growth as well. Is laziness keeping you from achieving what you want? Is the fear of failure one of your weaknesses? Are you too concerned about what others think? Are you afraid of conflict? Are you afraid of being with other people? Are you indecisive?

The more familiar you are with your weaknesses, the more empowered you will become to work through them and not allow them to keep you from reaching your potential. Recognizing and acknowledging your weaknesses is the first step toward acknowledging your strengths, which are your true allies in moving forward. Don't let your recognized weaknesses hold you back.

ME—I recognize my weaknesses in self-absorption, conflict avoidance, and denial. There are times when my acknowledged weaknesses are also strengths. Being self-absorbed allows me to dedicate myself to planning for what I want and going after it without delay. Avoiding conflicts allows for greater social acceptance among other people and gives me power to stay clear of people I do not particularly enjoy. Although I was steeped in denial about my relationships with my parents (a relationship I once perceived as made in heaven) it has never prevented me from obtaining what I wanted in a healthy way. Self-confidence and lack of concern (sometimes excessive) for what others think has always helped me achieve my goals.

YOU—

# WHENEVER YOU FALL

Whenever you fall, simply get back up. Equestrians who fall off their horses get right back in the saddle; baseball players who strike out take their next turn at the plate. Picking yourself up after a fall is as important mentally as it is physically.

If you're frustrated, or after you fail at something, don't stay on the ground, as tempting as this may be. We waste too much time on self pity, anger, and blame. Just brush yourself off and get ready for the next challenge, the changed direction, and the new path. By eliminating your fear of falling, you empower yourself to always move forward, with confidence and self-assuredness, knowing that whatever lies ahead is welcome because all life is a gift to be enjoyed.

ME—One of BARC's board members, Peter, was a very successful livestock auctioneer who once put together a classy horse show as a fundraiser. We invested countless hours in the effort. The day of the event was beautiful, but our turnout was very poor. Peter suggested that we not pay the vendors he'd hired in order to break even for the day. I didn't think this was right. In the end, BARC's first and last horse show lost $4,000. The other members of the board were not happy. Peter was embarrassed by the whole thing and eventually left the board, while I stayed on as Executive Director. Though we never held another horse show, we went on from this failure to stage many more successful fundraising events.

YOU—

# WHEREVER YOU GO BE KIND

Wherever you go, sow kindness. When you are kind, the world is a better place, and it returns to you in spades. Kindness spreads exponentially to every one around you, who in turn, spread it to everyone around them, and so on. When someone is kind to you, remember to be kind to someone else. Be generous by being considerate of others all the time in each and every moment.

ME—With the combination of my mother and father in me, it is difficult for me to be hateful and mean. The field of human services is imbued with kindness since anyone who makes a career helping and supporting others must have a kind heart. The true, lasting beauty of my career is founded on the memories of the culture of human kindness that BARC embraced: children hugging each other; ambulatory adults assisting the wheelchair bound; the mentally able respectfully enduring the behavior of the mentally disabled; parents volunteering for the greater good; staff preferring no pay raise to seeing others lose their jobs, and going out of their way to meet the needs of those with developmental disabilities.

YOU—

# WHETHER YOUR GOALS ARE BIG OR SMALL

Whether you goals are big or small does not matter. What is important is that you have goals. Allow the big goals to be your motivation and allow your smaller goals propel you forward. What you experience each day will forge your smaller goals and what you dream will create your bigger ones.

Small goals are important despite their size: How to manage a difficult co-worker or boss? How to accept your brother's radical views of the world? How to accept waiting in line? How to enjoy getting up in the morning? How to embrace each day with joy?

Your larger goals . . . how to grow your business, attain your career goal, overcome worry, accept who you are, confront your fear of public speaking, make peace with someone who dislikes you . . . are more sweeping and require time and thoughtful energy to obtain. By meeting the challenge posed by your smaller goals, one at a time, you empower yourself and gain confidence to meet the challenge of the larger, more complex goals.

ME—Learning to accept the vast differences in people was something that came easily to me since I enjoyed and was fascinated by the panorama of personalities. Accepting differing personalities has allowed me to meet small goals on many occasions: dealing with difficult co-workers, an ornery boss, accepting unpleasant salespeople, getting along with members of my family. I found that accepting differing personalities was also a critical ingredient in attaining my larger goals: staying employed at BARC, growing the agency, having a successful and happy career.

YOU—

# WORDS ARE IMPORTANT

Words need to be carefully chosen, crafted and spoken. While it's true that words can't break your bones like sticks and stones, according to the familiar taunt, they can cause irreparable harm to yourself and others. Paying careful attention to your thoughts, words, time, and actions is the first step to living a more rewarding and fulfilling existence, and being more appreciative of all that life has to offer.

ME—I can think of a number of occasions when I regretted the words I used. Twice I asked big-bellied women when their due dates were; both were not pregnant. I am very sorry that as a young man, with absolutely no forethought or sensitivity, I told my sister Lynne that she did not need nose surgery since her naturally sized nose was part of who she was. My unthinking comment caused her much unnecessary anxiety about her decision; fortunately, she had the operation and looks and feels much better for it. When Shirley's brother died and we were shopping for coffins, without any forethought or sensitivity, I asked her what her preference would be for herself. Regrettably, the first thing I once said to the man who'd just won BARC's Mercedes Benz Raffle was that any donation to BARC would be very appreciated. Time has helped heal my regrettable words, and I have learned to use more forethought and sensitivity before opening my mouth.

YOU—

# WORKING IS IMPORTANT

Work is the opiate of life. Have you ever noticed that when you are busy, you always feel better at the end of day, no matter how tired you are, than when you have nothing to do? Movement and work are what make life happen. Lethargy and stagnation make life more difficult. Challenge is the spice of life, not the bane of existence. Without challenge, we have no choice, and without choice, we have no life.

Living is about choosing the road to take, the path to follow, the direction to go. Life is not about stillness and having everything provided, as it was in the Garden of Eden. We were created in G-d's image not because we look like G-d, but because, like G-d, we have choice.

ME—BARC employs nearly three hundred handicapped workers in two sheltered workshops who perform subcontract work for private industry. Over the years, the highest incidence of behavioral problems occurred whenever we had limited subcontract work. Whenever we were busy and bustling with deadlines to meet, the incidence of behavioral outbreaks was always lower.

YOU—

# YOU ARE ALIVE

You are alive not to take and impress but to give and award. You are here to question, answer, explore, imagine, and do. You are not here to worry and fret about all the things you have no control over anyway.

Bring joy to wherever you go and do not react to circumstances. You make your own circumstances and can choose to change those that discourage, or bring you and others down. Even the most difficult situations have the potential for joy and gratitude. Be the messenger and role model of that joy and gratitude.

By judging a circumstance that others find dreadful in a positive light, you shine that light on everything and everyone. You can apply your positive light in all circumstances . . . at home, at work, and with others.

ME—I took all I could from my parents: their wisdom, values, money, caring, love, food and shelter. I gave all I could to my sons: my wisdom, my values, my money, my caring, my love, my food and shelter. My parents awarded me with their genetic makeup and with the way they raised and treated me. I awarded my sons by giving myself to them. I do all I can every day to be grateful to others. Much of my gratitude derives from being with others, conversing with them, and learning from them.

YOU—

# YOU DESERVE THE BEST

You deserve the best life has to offer, so today, do something just for you. Taking care of you is not selfishness because the better you are, the better you will be for everyone else.

When you take care of yourself, you are better equipped to care and take care of others. On airplanes, passengers with children are always instructed to take care of themselves first by putting on their oxygen mask, if the need arises, and then attending to their children. A parent dizzy from lack of oxygen will not be of much help to a child struggling to put on his or her oxygen mask. When you take care of yourself, your light shines more brightly for everyone else. When you take care of yourself, you and the world become better. By caring for yourself, you become more effective, more productive, and more the kind of person who can make a positive difference.

ME—When I started taking care of myself and doing the things that I wanted to do, I not only became more joyful but I also was much more appreciated by others. Eating in gourmet restaurants is an absolutely magnificent experience as is regular full body massages. Sipping top shelf liquors and smoking aged hand rolled cigars, especially with very good friends, is quite heavenly. Listening to the world's finest symphony orchestras and opera companies connects my spirit with a universal consciousness. Just sitting outdoors and enjoying all the sights, sounds, smells, and sensations is a free gift that I take advantage of as often as possible.

YOU—

# YOU HAVE THE POWER

You have the power to change the world simply by being the best you can be. Your positive energy, if you allow it, illuminates the rest of the world and everyone around you; it infuses others with hope and joy.

Only you are capable of making who you are and your life better. Only you can improve yourself and in the process change the world. Your light can easily become your own reward as you reach your highest goals. Along the way, you'll positively influence everyone and everything you come in contact with. You have the power to change and it is your most wonderful gift.

ME—Unfortunately, just as I reach the apex of my career, I am close to retirement. Through all the years as I journeyed to this point, I have changed dramatically for the better. Of course, I have not changed the external world around me . . . that goes on as it always has. What has changed, through my change, is the way I handle and counsel staff about the exigencies of the day . . . personnel, legal, financial, people supported and volunteer issues. Because I am comfortable with who I am, my staff can better cope with the myriad of issues that arise. I know and live the Talmudic wisdom that to change the life of one person is like changing the whole world.

YOU—

# YOUR CAPABILITIES

Your capabilities are too extensive to write down . . . so don't. If you can appreciate a fraction of your G-d-given blessings, then you are ready to fill each moment of your day with exuberance and powerful energy.

Your blessings are not secrets; they are always there, right in front of you. Maybe you're handy with a hammer; maybe you can whistle a tune or plant a beautiful garden. All of these gifts bring pleasure to others, and to you. Grab them, adore them, worship them, and use them. When you become fully alive, you are immersed in joy, gratitude, positive energy, richness, and awe.

ME—Each year I become more appreciative of my capabilities. I have never been exceptionally handy around the house but it has never prevented me from the joy of fixing things. I rarely am able to whistle or sing on key but it has never prevented me from whistling and humming. I even sing, whenever I am alone and beyond the hearing range of others. I still enjoy planting things and watching them grow. Every year I wedge several birdhouses between some backyard crossbeams and the roof of the house and take great pleasure in watching aviary couples make their selection, furnish their dwelling with debris, lay their eggs, and feed their young until they are able to fly off on their own. I truly appreciate my capabilities and the equally incredible capabilities of life all around me.

YOU—

# YOUR DREAMS

Your dreams can come to life, no matter how far away they may seem. In fact, some of our closest dreams remain unattainable. It all depends on the path you take. If the movie you want to see is playing at a theater that's a mile to the east of where you live, that's very close by but you will never reach it if you drive in a westerly direction.

Likewise, your dreams will never be realized if you are traveling on the wrong path, or in the wrong direction. Set your direction and path in the same direction as your dreams. Then, create a plan, and be patient. Follow the plan with determination, courage and enthusiasm, and you will realize your dreams. Do not let the daily frustrations and distractions of living deter you from the bigger picture . . . the dream of your highest vision.

ME—I had two unrealistic dreams . . . of being a professional baseball player and a messianic leader. I could have been a professional baseball player with a lot of effort, but I lacked the motivation to play one hundred and sixty-two games every year. I knew this since I was tired and lost interest when I played forty-two games each summer in my semi-professional league. I left my baseball career in my early twenties to attend graduate school and pursue my evolving dream of becoming a successful human services administrator. The messianic leader rumination was a metaphor for leadership.

YOU—

# YOUR EXPECTATIONS

Your expectations govern your reality. If you expect little, you will receive little; but if you expect great things, then you will need to commit yourself to achieving at a high standard. Only low expectations are achieved with no effort. If you have high expectations, you'll have to work.

If you set your expectations high, you will live more fully, with more challenge, more opportunity, and more gusto. Along the way, you will also encounter many obstacles and frustrations. Take each one as it comes and move forward confidently, even if you have to change your approach. Regardless of how high your expectations, they are always achievable. It's just a matter of time and your will.

ME—In midlife I was aroused by a colleague to pursue a doctorate in public administration. Returning to school as a lowly student after being in charge of a significant nonprofit organization for many years was not easy. Even at the doctoral level I encountered my share of professors who left no doubt as to who was in charge. I soon discovered that achieving a doctoral degree was a very high expectation since only about 25% of all doctoral students actually receive their degrees. Undeterred I plodded forward over the course of eight years, jumping over many hurdles and through many hoops. After my course work I successfully sat for two all day comprehensive exams only to discover myself in the final and most difficult hoop: proposing, researching, writing and defending my dissertation. Through much patience and determination I received my doctoral degree.

YOU—

# YOUR EYES

Your eyes see the world through your filter. If ten people observe the same event, they will report ten different versions of the event. Likewise, where some people look at a situation and see gloom and doom, others see hope and opportunity.

Whatever you see in other people is in you. To see and feel pain, you need the experience of pain. To see beauty, you need to understand beauty. The purveyors of despair see the world as a dark, foreboding place. The believers, who shine bright in joy and happiness, see the world as a bright, magnificent place, a gift for all to enjoy. The world you see is a reflection of how you feel. How you feel will filter your interpretation of what you see and experience.

ME—My eyes have seen the world from several different angles: from the deep, dark caverns of hopelessness to the pinnacle of the highest mountain, and from the gray plateau that lies between them. I now know it is all about attitude. When I was hopeless, the world was hopeless. When I was flying high, the world was a magnificent place. In my moments between hopelessness and hope, the world was just what it always was . . . the world. The world does not judge, it just is. Human beings judge; that's why I have learned to do all I can to give my judgments a positive spin for my own sake and the sake of everyone I contact.

YOU—

# YOUR INFLUENCE

Your influence on the world can come from protesting wars, signing petitions, or working against injustice. However, your greatest influence generally will be seen much closer to home because it comes from your heart, in your everyday interactions with other people.

Influence one person with your positive, life affirming energy, and you will have influenced the entire world. Redirect your worries and concerns toward a positive, productive end and you will move yourself and others into the world of joy and happiness. There are many more things you can achieve than there are things you can worry about. Where you put your energy is up to you; put it to good use.

ME—In my twenties, I spent hours discussing and dissecting national and international events, and taking positions on issues of the day. Over time, I realized as an ordinary American citizen, my opinions held little sway. No matter how brilliant my analysis or insight, what I thought wouldn't necessarily influence anyone or create change in the world at large. What really mattered in my life were the events much closer to home . . . my parents, my wife, my children, my partner, my friends, my associates at work, and the people I supported through my work. When I started to exert my energy toward events in my "closer to home" world, I began living more happily and effectively.

YOU—

# YOUR LIFE'S DIRECTION

Your life will go in whatever direction you decide. When you concentrate and focus your attention on something you want, then you make it happen. The very moment you start attending to your desires, you begin to fulfill that desire.

If you care about doing as little as possible for yourself or other people, then, with very little effort, you will succeed at it. If you care about watching television, then, with very little effort, you will succeed at it. If you care about being with other people and making a difference in your life and theirs, then, with effort, you will succeed. Take an inventory about what you care about most, and become fully aware of what it is; then start making it happen.

ME—My life has taken a very common and linear direction. I grew up with both my parents and graduated high school before going on to college and graduate school and getting married at age twenty-five. My wife and I raised two fine sons and my career moved up the ladder of success with at least five employers before securing my current position with BARC. Today I am still on a linear path with my sons both living independently as I plan for my retirement. Some of my current desires require very little effort such as watching movies or listening to music. Other desires require a lot more effort such as socializing and continuing to succeed at work.

YOU—

# YOUR POTENTIAL

Your potential is infinite. Reach beyond where you are and when you get there, keep reaching for more. It is not a question of quantity; it is a matter of quality. The more quality you have in your life, the more joy and happiness you bring to yourself and the universe.

Always reaching for your highest potential is gratifying in itself, whether or not you are successful, because the act of reaching itself will bring you much joy and satisfaction and improve the quality of life for everyone around you. Be the winner you were always meant to be by making the effort with purpose and passion. Living fully does not mean that you always have to win and succeed; it means that you have to always strive for the best life has to offer.

ME—I have always been equipped with an oversized ego, so I never had any problem or insecurity about going after what I wanted. In recent years, the potential that I have been pursuing is daily joy. I believe my potential for daily joy is without boundary. I am very satisfied and content as I write these words, and I know that even higher satisfactions and more contentment are possible. I intend to spend the rest of my life in pursuit of these higher pleasures. I do not know what height I will attain but I do know that I aspire for the infinite . . . and that life is about journey, not the achievement.

YOU—

# YOUR VIEW

Your view of what you need will determine how happy and fulfilled you are. If your view is that you have to get up and go to work so you can pay the rent, then you may be restricting yourself to a life without joy and meaning, a life of drudgery. What if you got up excited about all the new day will bring and how you will add value to your life and the world? This is really living.

Take a positive, joyful view of the world and you can change daily drudgery into smiles and pleasure. If your view of what you need is money and fame, you may find, once achieving them, that they are empty. Enjoying life comes from enjoying the simple things . . . the sunrises and sunsets, a full moon, the change of seasons, the miracle of our breath, a gorgeous flower. Money, fame, and prestige do not have anything to do with inner joy and happiness; they are all fleeting externalities that do nothing for your inner joy.

ME—All I need is food, shelter, nature, and other people. To me, everything else is an accoutrement. I do cherish my automobile for the freedom it offers, but fashionable clothing, expensive jewelry, fashionable furnishings, art, toys, and speedy computers are all unnecessary luxuries. Of all the people I know who have died, none took their possessions with them to the grave. Those to whom they bequeathed their possessions often sold these items for cash. What we cherish and remember is a person's spirit, a person's point of view. That stays with us forever.

YOU—

# ZOOMING TO DESTINY

Zooming to your destiny, or approaching it with baby steps... the means of achieving your dreams is totally dependent on you. Some of us dive right into the water; others wade in a toe at a time. All that differs is our style.

What I hope you have learned in these pages is that all you ever needed has always been available to you. You can achieve whatever you want immediately by simply starting to use your gifts.

To reach the unreachable is very doable; it simply requires that you take stock of who you are, and take action. It will not happen if your destiny and dreams remain in the realm of fantasy. It will happen only if you begin to consciously take action in whatever direction you want to go.

ME—I certainly did not zoom to my destiny; for me, the process was more of a long, drawn-out drifting. When I finally realized who I was and what gifts had always been available to me, I was able to start doing, to start really living and appreciating what I had. Like many others, I found that realizing my gifts was only half the battle; I still had to change old, ingrained, counterproductive habits. It took a full five years for me to let go of my nonproductive fantasies and start living each day as the person I always was, with a full appreciation of each moment and all of life's gifts.

YOU—

# MAY PEACE AND JOY BE WITH YOU

I cannot end this book without expressing my very deep heartfelt love for my soul mate, Jean, who has given me unimaginable guidance to discover who I had always been. I cannot express in words the incredible delight I have living with someone that is so meant for me, my true *"Bashert"*. As a person who enjoys his time alone, to live with someone who honors time alone is a true blessing. She is someone who understands the critical importance of being true to one's self; she allows me to fail and achieve as I see appropriate.

I sincerely hope you have enjoyed reading and documenting your journey throughout these pages. It has been a wonderful experience for me, and like so much in my life, has provided me with new insights about who I am and where I am going. Please remember to take care of yourself! Taking care of yourself is best accomplished by being yourself and doing things that give you and others pleasure and joy!